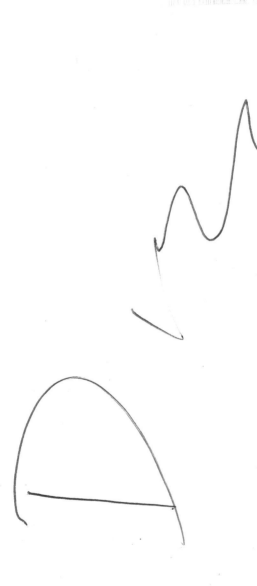

IT'S ROCK 'N' ROLL

Even if you don't remember such names as the Drifters, the Penguins, and Bill Haley and the Comets, you can't miss the new popularity of the music and style of the 1950s. Sha-Na-Na, John Travolta, *Grease*, and *Happy Days* are just a few of the results of the rock 'n' roll revival today. This comprehensive look at the fabulous fifties tells you about the important musicians, dances, styles of dress, and social climate of the times. The causes of the current movement and its present style setters are also examined in detail. You'll be finger snapping to the tunes of Chuck Berry, Buddy Holly, and the Coasters along with the fifties enthusiasts around the country.

Gene Busnar

It's Rock

'n' Roll

JULIAN MESSNER New York

To Elizabeth, without whose help and love
this book could not have been written

For permission to reprint lyrics, we thank Bobby Robinson for "The Closer
You Are," *Spinning Wheel Music*, and for "Ya-Ya," *Fast Music*.

Copyright © 1979 by Gene Busnar
Second Printing, 1980
All rights reserved
including the right of reproduction
in whole or in part in any form
Published by Julian Messner
A Simon & Schuster Division of
Gulf & Western Corporation
Simon & Schuster Building
1230 Avenue of the Americas
New York, New York 10020

Julian Messner and
Colophon are trademarks
of Simon & Schuster,
registered in the U.S.
Patent and Trademark Office.

Designed by Irving Perkins

Manufactured in the United States of America

Library of Congress Cataloging in Publication Data
Busnar, Gene.
It's rock 'n' roll.
Includes index.
1. Rock music—United States—History and criticism.
I. Title.
ML3561.R62B9   784   79-10927
ISBN 0-671-32977-4

Also available in Wanderer Paperback edition

Contents

ACKNOWLEDGMENTS

I would like to thank all the people connected with early rock 'n' roll and the fifties revival who helped me with this project. Special thanks to Bobby Robinson, Billy Vera, Ray Reneri, Don K. Reed, Len Lopate, and Paul Sherman ("the crown prince of rock 'n' roll"). This book was greatly enriched by the picture collections of "Bleecker" Bob Plotnik, Billy Vera, Record World Magazine, and Neal Hollander of Banner Talent Agency.

A number of friends contributed in various ways to the completion of this book. These include Kathryn Lance, Elaine Landau, David Siegel, John Sposato, Mark Schimmel, Paul Brown, Arnie Alpert, Susan Lipschitz, Dave Alexander, John Kois, and the Sugermans.

Finally, I would like to thank my wife Liz for all her work and contribution to this book. Special thanks to my parents, Mr. and Mrs. Irving Busnar, for their moral support. Last, but certainly not least, I would like to thank my editor, Iris Rosoff for her patience and understanding throughout this project.

The Fifties: Then and Now

Sha Na Na (Courtesy of Kama Sutra Records)

The Rock 'n' Roll Revival

The first major rock 'n' roll revival concert was held at New York's Felt Forum in late 1969. Richard Nader, the show's producer, felt that the musical trends of the sixties had peaked with the Woodstock rock festival. He sensed a gap in the music scene and decided to fill that gap with fifties rock 'n' roll music. His first step was to try to find as many popular fifties acts as possible. This was no easy task, since many of these performers had been out of the music business for years. The members of even the most popular groups had long since gone their separate ways. But when the word got out that the oldies were again in demand, Nader was flooded with phone calls from rock 'n' roll hit makers of the past. The performers who worked that first show included Chuck Berry, Bill Haley and the Comets, the Coasters, and the Platters.

The Felt Forum concert was not a total success. Many of the old groups had only one or two of the original members, while other performers simply lacked the magic that they had had in the fifties. In some cases, a singer resented having to sing old hits. Although the concert was billed as an oldies show, these performers wanted to sing contemporary music. The crowd, however, wanted to hear only the early hits. They were pleased with the Shirelles and the Comets, who ran off oldie after oldie with the energy that had made these acts popular in the first place. But the performers who excited the crowd the most were a group of ten former students from Columbia University called Sha Na Na. This group had

Flash Cadillac and the Continental Kids (Courtesy of *Record World* magazine)

never made records in the fifties, but as they recreated the songs they grew up with, much of the audience began dancing in the aisles.

Sha Na Na did not simply sing the oldies. They dressed and acted in the style of tough-looking fifties teenagers. Although Sha Na Na never had a hit record, they became tremendously popular at concerts. For the most part, their versions of the oldies could not compare with the original records. But the group's success has always hinged more on their style than their sound. Their duck-tail haircuts and black leather jackets recall an era when teenagers did nothing but hang out on the corner, watch the girls go by, and sing "doo-wop" songs like "Earth Angel" and "Get a Job." One of the nonsense lyrics in the latter song was "sha-na-na-na-na-na-na-na-na," and that is how the group got its name.

Their act began during the student demonstrations in the late sixties. There was a great deal of tension on the Columbia campus, and the students decided that a little taste of the fifties would help lighten things up. While the music of the late sixties reflected the seriousness of the times, fifties rock 'n' roll had a simpler and more direct appeal. The Columbia audience loved Sha Na Na; the group's career was launched.

The popularity of Sha Na Na did not go unnoticed by others in the entertainment business. One of the most important events in the launching of the new fifties craze was the opening on Broadway in 1971 of the play *Grease*. The setting for *Grease* is an urban high school in the late fifties. The characters are all dressed in typical fifties style: the girls in tight sweaters and pony tails and the boys in motorcycle jackets and greasy long hair. Everybody talks in typical fifties lingo and sings songs which are spoofs of fifties rock 'n' roll hits. *Grease* has become Broadway's longest running musical and has also done well in other cities around the country. One Los Angeles production of the play in the early seventies featured a then-unknown actor, John Travolta. He has since gone on to become one of the superstars of the late seventies.

There is something in Travolta's style which seems to bridge the gap between the fifties and the seventies. Even the hit movie *Saturday Night Fever* has an atmosphere that is much like the earlier decade. Although the music in this movie is in the current disco style, Travolta and his friends look and act much like the greasers

John Travolta with the producers of *Grease* (Courtesy of *Grease*, Broadway's longest running musical)

of the fifties. This connection is made even clearer in the 1978 movie version of *Grease*. Music and styles from the past and present are mixed so thoroughly that the seventies and fifties seem to become one.

Shortly after *Grease* opened on Broadway, several movies were made about the fifties. One of these was *Let the Good Times Roll*. The movie mixed film clips of popular early rock 'n' roll performers as they were in the fifties and as they appeared in concert during a seventies revival tour. In addition, there was footage of related incidents and important people during rock 'n' roll's early years. The movie is the best documentary of the fifties revival to date.

The most influential revival movie of the early seventies, *American Graffiti*, starred Richard Dreyfus, Ron Howard, Cindy Williams, and Candy Clark and featured the popular disc jockey, Wolfman Jack. The movie inspired several television spin-offs:

"Happy Days" and "Laverne and Shirley." Not surprisingly, these shows starred Ron Howard and Cindy Williams in roles that were similar to the ones they played in *American Graffiti*. The most popular TV greaser of the seventies is the "Fonz," as portrayed by Henry Winkler in "Happy Days."

Like the characters in Sha Na Na, Fonzie is an overgrown teen-ager who is mainly concerned with talking cool and looking slick. In one particularly funny episode of "Happy Days," the Fonz re-fuses to take off his boots at the beach. While everyone else is jumping into the water, Fonzie is sitting on a blanket wearing only his bathing suit and motorcycle boots. His only worry in life seems to be keeping his duck-tail neat and his car running fast.

Because of ABC's success with "Happy Days" and "Laverne and Shirley," Sha Na Na got its own weekly variety show on NBC. The show proved to be so popular in 1976 that the network ex-tended its run for an additional two years. The guys sing and dance, as well as perform skits with a weekly guest. Most of the guests are well-known performers from the early rock 'n' roll

The girls from *Grease* (Courtesy of *Grease*, Broadway's longest running musical)

years. Oldies' concert producer Ray Reneri feels that Sha Na Na's TV show gives the oldies concerts a big boost. Oldies performers get exposure on national television, while Sha Na Na's singing of the old hits helps familiarize young people with this music. Reneri, who currently produces the annual revival shows at New York's Madison Square Garden, is amazed at the way today's teenagers respond to the oldies:

> When we put on the first revival shows in '69, the audience was mostly people who grew up in the fifties. But that has all changed in the last few years. The audiences are mostly kids.

Wolfman Jack (Neal Hollander Collection)

A Fonz look-alike and some of his friends (Courtesy of *Grease*, Broadway's longest running musical)

They seem to know the words to every popular oldie. If a name group like the Shirelles don't do one of their hits, the kids demand it. I think the reason for this great response is the words to the songs. In most modern rock music, the playing is so loud that it is impossible to know what the lyrics are. Of course, the rock 'n' roll revival is helped greatly by Travolta, and TV shows like "Happy Days," "Laverne and Shirley," and "Sha Na Na."

Many radio stations have also become aware of the changing tastes of their listeners. Some have adopted a policy of program-

The Five Satins ("Bleecker" Bob Plotnik Collection)

ming only songs from the fifties and sixties. WCBS-FM in New York was one station that moved to this kind of a format in the early seventies. Today, the station plays some current hits, but relies heavily on older records.

A 1977 listeners' poll of the top 500 records of all time provided some interesting results. Seven of the top ten all-time favorites were songs from the fifties. The top three songs on this survey were by vocal groups from the mid-fifties: "In the Still of the Night," the Five Satins (1956); "Earth Angel," the Penguins (1955); and "Tonight Tonight," the Mellow Kings (1957). Another survey taken by this station indicated that over half of its listeners are teenagers. Disc jockey Don K. Reed, who hosts a weekly oldies show called the "Doo-wop Shop," feels that early vocal group rock 'n' roll is most popular in New York, Chicago, Philadelphia, and Los Angeles. But Joey Dee, of "Peppermint Twist" fame, has performed all over the country and claims that "the old songs are popular in all areas." Ray Reneri recalls, however, that this was not always the case.

> Oldies were always very popular in New York, although the first revival concerts didn't make a lot of money. But for the last four or five years, oldies have been popular wherever you look—Buffalo, Toronto, Cleveland, etc. In foreign countries, the music is even more popular. England, Holland, Germany, and even Japan are places where early rock 'n' roll performers are in great demand. In fact, the State Department recently requested the Shirelles and Chubby Checker tour the Communist nations of Eastern Europe. So you can see how popular this music has become.

Most insiders agree that many oldies groups are only popular locally. A group like the Harptones or the Cleftones work mostly on the East Coast, while the Dells and Moonglows are best known in the Midwest. Two of the more famous groups, the Coasters and the Drifters, have had so many members over the years that there are at least two versions of each group performing in various parts of the country. Each group contains several original members along with a few newcomers. The current rule of thumb is that a group must contain two original members in order to work major concerts.

An interesting twist to the revival story is that some performers dislike being associated with their old records. They take it as an insult that their past songs are more in demand than their current music. The most famous case in point is Ricky Nelson. During the 1969 revival show in New York, Ricky did not want to perform his hits from the late fifties and early sixties. Instead, he preferred more current material like the Rolling Stones' "Honky Tonk Women." When the crowd began booing Nelson's choice of material, he finally gave in and sang a few of his old hits. He was quite depressed to find that the audience had no interest in his current musical tastes. In response, he wrote the song, "Garden Party," which became his first hit in many years. Several other performers have also gotten a negative response when they would not do their familiar hits. But the company that produces the revival shows now requires a performer to agree in writing to perform the songs for which he or she is best known.

Alan Freed with a New York vocal group—Lillian Leech and the Mellows ("Bleecker" Bob Plotnik Collection)

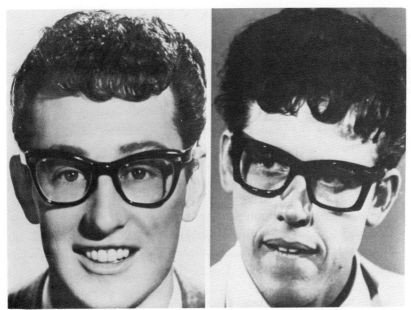

The real Buddy Holly (*left*) and Gary Busey in the title role of *The Buddy Holly Story* (Courtesy of Columbia Pictures)

At the present time, oldies are so popular that many name performers work this circuit. The most successful ones, like Fats Domino, the Shirelles, and Chuck Berry, do almost nothing else. Some other artists now perform primarily in other musical styles, but they do appear at the large revival concerts. For example, Jerry Lee Lewis had been a popular country performer for almost twenty years. But he is so well remembered for his rock 'n' roll records of the fifties that he rarely misses a major revival show. Many of the smaller acts work regularly in clubs, although they must usually supplement their earnings with day jobs. Other popular acts from the fifties have not been able to find a place on the revival circuit. Many of them seemed to lose their touch after not performing day jobs for years. Others had taken other work and had no desire to reenter the music business.

The recent popularity of early rock 'n' roll spawned several movies in the late seventies. The 1978 film, *American Hot Wax*, attempts to tell the story of disc jockey Alan Freed. The movie actually captures the feeling of the Brooklyn Paramount's rock 'n' roll shows of the fifties. Along with appearances by Chuck Berry and Jerry Lee Lewis, there are several fictionalized groups in the movie: the Chesterfields (supposedly Frankie Lymon and the Teenagers) and the Planetones (supposedly the Del Vikings). Different aspects of Freed's personality are glimpsed—his sincere love of the music, his drinking problem, and his rapid-fire delivery on the radio. Although the feeling of the music and the excitement of Freed's live shows are accurately presented, one does not walk out of the theater with any real understanding of what the man was like.

Another 1978 rock 'n' roll film, *The Buddy Holly Story*, stars Gary Busey in the title role. The movie begins in a small town in Texas, where Buddy and his band are working a local skating rink. The band is playing traditional popular and country tunes of the day, which are being broadcast over a local radio station. When Holly begins playing rock 'n' roll, the kids go wild. At the same time, the radio show's sponsors object to "that sinful music." The group is fired, but success is just around the corner. The movie then traces the group's road to fame and fortune up until the time of Holly's untimely death in a plane crash. Several members of this group, the Crickets, complain that *The Buddy Holly Story* misrepresents certain facts about the singer's life; nevertheless, the movie does capture the general flavor of the times and is worth seeing.

Buddy Holly and his band as portrayed by Gary Busey and co-stars Don Stroud and Charley Martin Smith (Courtesy of Columbia Pictures)

FIFTIES NOSTALGIA

The dictionary defines nostalgia as, "a longing for something far away or long ago." There has always been nostalgia for past eras. Music and styles from decades gone by often make a comeback years later. The seventies have seen a tremendous amount of nostalgia for the fifties. Some observers feel that this is caused by a vacuum in the seventies. Most people in the field of music would agree that the seventies are not a very rich period for rock music.

The fifties are usually described as a period that was boring and unexciting. In contrast, the sixties are remembered as a decade when many political and social problems came to light. Early rock 'n' roll music held a great deal of excitement for young people in the fifties, but the music was not at all concerned with social problems. This all changed in the mid-sixties. As people's lives became more complicated, so did popular music. Many of the problems that came to light in the sixties are still not resolved, and many people would just as soon forget them. In this sense, the seventies are much like the fifties. There certainly were problems in the fifties—the H-bomb tests, the quiz show and payola scandals, the House Un-American Activities Committee, the space race, and the Communist spy scares. Yet the fifties are usually pictured as a carefree time.

A child of the seventies gives his portrayal of a fifties greaser.

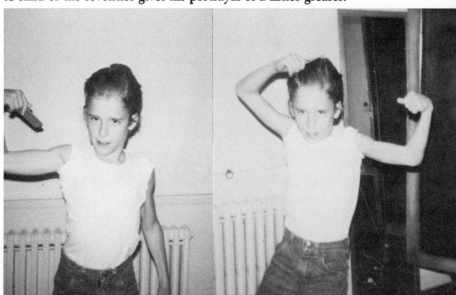

When *Grease* and *American Graffiti* became successful in the early seventies, there were many articles written about fifties nostalgia. One article in *Life* magazine in 1973 noted: "Pop psychologists and many of the kids see the flight to the fifties as a search for a happier time before drugs, Vietnam and assassinations." In the same article, Dick Biondi, a Chicago disc jockey, was quoted as saying that through the revival of fifties music, "Kids are finding a backdoor way of getting together with their parents." In another article which appeared in the *New York Times* in 1973, Biondi observed, "My audience wants to forget its problems and return to—or at least recall those happy high school times—the prom, no wars, no riots, no protests, the convertible at the drive-in." Another DJ, Boston's "Little" Walter Devanne, told a reporter for *Newsweek:* "It's like the early sixties when there was the first big oldies craze, because there was a big lull in the music, and people were waiting for something to happen. Finally, the Beatles came along in 1964. We are in the same lull now, and the fifties are filling in."

Performers in oldies groups feel much the same way as Biondi and Devanne. One member of the revival group, the Belmonts, traces the revival to a desire for a music that is fun. "During the late sixties, popular music got so serious and wordy. I think people got tired of it pretty quickly. People want to be entertained by music, not depressed." Joey Dee put it even more simply. "The kids want to be able to dance and sing along with the lyrics. That's not easy to do with a lot of current rock. A lot of the kids are still too young to get into discos, so they turn to the oldies." Guitar player Billy Vera, who backs up many oldies performers, has a different explanation. "Rock 'n' roll belongs to kids, it's their music. That's why they're interested in its past."

A major event in the revival of fifties music was the death of Elvis Presley in 1977. Almost immediately, the sales of Elvis's records multiplied tremendously. There have been several Elvis conventions and thousands of people have spent large sums on rare pictures and records of "the King." There also have been many Presley imitators since his death. On a recent Dick Clark TV show, ten of them appeared on stage together.

The fifties revival has become a multimillion-dollar business. It has been so successful that promoters have tried to revive other musical eras. One example is the hit show *Beatlemania.* As the ads say, "It's not the Beatles, but an incredible simulation." Because many people never saw the Beatles together, they are willing to settle for a good imitation. The show's producer found four musicians who sounded like, and, in some cases, looked like, the Beatles.

During the summer of 1978, the movie *Sgt. Pepper's Lonely Heart's Club Band,* starring Peter Frampton and the Bee Gees, was released. The film did not receive good reviews and the music was clearly inferior to the orginal Beatles' records. Still, many people will mistakenly buy the movie soundtrack rather than the authentic recordings. There is a danger here. The Beatles' music is among the greatest in the history of rock. When too many imitations become available, listeners often get directed away from the originals. Of course, producers and musicians have a right to imitate whomever they want. At the same time, listeners deserve to hear the best music available.

The chapters that follow attempt to tell the true story of rock 'n' roll. The music grew up in the fifties and early sixties. The best performers and records of the rock 'n' roll era will be looked at. By understanding the development of music and the events that brought it about, it is hoped that the joy of listening to fifties rock 'n' roll will be increased.

The Way It Really Was

When people look back, they tend to recall only the good times. The fifties, in particular, are remembered as trouble-free and happy years. Nostalgia buffs like to talk about fads like the hula hoop, duck-tail haircuts, 3-D movies, and cramming twenty-one college students into a phone booth. These humorous crazes were a big part of growing up in the fifties. But there were also many serious problems during those years. The Korean War, Senator Joseph McCarthy's indictment of many innocent people, the civil rights struggle, and the cold war with Russia were just some of the events that laid the groundwork for the explosive decade to follow. Meanwhile, a new generation of young people was seeking out its freedom.

Teenagers began to emerge as a distinct social group shortly after World War II. For the first time, society was affluent enough to allow most thirteen- to nineteen-year-olds to postpone going to work. Unlike past generations, teenagers of the fifties were not overgrown children or miniature adults. They had evolved into a distinct group struggling to define themselves and create their own culture. By the mid-fifties, rock 'n' roll had become the cornerstone of that culture.

The music that eventually came to be called rock 'n' roll was originally called rhythm and blues (R&B). Until the fifties, this music had been almost exclusively recorded by black performers for black audiences. But in the early fifties, a growing number of white teenagers had become interested in R&B. By 1954, this group had grown large enough to have its tastes reflected in the hit parade surveys. Around the same time, the Supreme Court ordered integration of schools and buses in the South. It is perhaps more than a coincidence that both blacks and young whites were seeking greater freedom during the early and mid-fifties. The emergence of rock 'n' roll during those years seemed to represent a coming together of these two groups.

THE MUSIC SCENE IN THE EARLY FIFTIES

Before 1954, there were three more or less distinct areas of popular music: pop, country, and rhythm and blues (also called "race music"). Although there were occasional crossovers from one area into another, the three fields were generally isolated. Each area of music had its own record companies and performers. Most radio stations featured only one type of popular music, and audiences knew which ones catered to their tastes. For the most part, listeners and artists could easily distinguish one kind of popular music from another. The emergence of rock 'n' roll broke down these barriers as elements from the three musical types became integrated.

Of the three musical fields, the pop segment was the biggest. It had the largest audience and was broadcast by more radio stations than the other types of popular music. In addition, the pop field was controlled by the four largest record companies, RCA, Columbia, Decca, and Mercury. These companies were known as the "majors." Each of these companies was a large corporation, with many interests outside the popular music fields. They also had well established connections in radio and television and could bring national attention to a new record within a short period of time.

The type of music that characterized the pop field was ballads and novelty songs. Usually these records featured a subdued beat and smooth singing. Although many of the most popular songs were about love, the topic was handled in a dramatic or sentimental way.

In contrast, many R&B records had a pounding beat and spoke directly about physical and emotional love. The rhythm and blues field was basically made up of black artists who recorded on small independent labels. These labels were known as "indies" in the music business. For the most part, the indies sold only to black audiences in certain regions of the country. Black artists understood that their sales were limited to black audiences. There were several exceptions to this rule, however—Nat King Cole, the Ink Spots, and the Mills Brothers, among others. But these artists sounded white. They did not use the traditions of black music in their work and were, therefore, totally acceptable to white listeners.

With the emergence of rock 'n' roll, a couple of the indies— namely, Atlantic and Imperial—grew as large as the majors. But most of the indies remained small throughout the rock 'n' roll era. Although most of these companies did not have the money or promotional facilities to compete with the majors, many records by these small companies became national hits. In spite of this, critics of rock 'n' roll often accused record companies and disc jockeys of forcing the music on the public. The truth is that the indies were able to have hits because listeners went out of their way to find these records. By the mid-fifties, the records on these small labels were reaching a large national audience.

The country and western field of popular music was the least affected by the coming of rock 'n' roll. Compared to R&B, country music was familiar to the mass audience. Most people had heard singing cowboys like Roy Rogers and Gene Autry in the movies and on TV. Occasionally, a popular C&W artist like Hank Williams would have a pop hit. Although country music had a regional quality, it was not offensive to most pop listeners. In addition, many of the most popular C&W artists were recorded by the majors. There were very few crossovers from the other fields onto the C&W charts. In the mid-fifties, country-rock performers like Elvis, Jerry Lee Lewis, and Carl Perkins did have country hits. But these artists were also authentic country performers. It was quite rare to find a pop or R&B artist on the C&W charts. Even a popular rock 'n' roller like Jerry Lee Lewis has stopped recording rock in order to maintain his standing with the C&W audience.

THE FIRST ROCK 'N' ROLL HIT

There is some disagreement as to what the first rock 'n' roll record was. The term *rock 'n' roll* had been used in black music for many years to describe physical sex. In the late forties, there was an instrumental R&B record called "Rock 'n' Roll" by Wild Bill Moore and his band. Many other records of that era used the term, although disc jockey Alan Freed is often credited with inventing it. Freed simply called the R&B records he played "rock 'n' roll." In time, the term came to mean those records which became pop-

The Chords ("Bleecker" Bob Plotnik Collection)

ular among white teenagers. By then, the music had taken on some of its own attributes and could often be distinguished from R&B.

The first R&B records to become pop hits were "Sh-Boom" by the Chords and "Gee" by the Crows, both in 1954. Although the Crows' record reached the charts first, "Sh-Boom" became a bigger and more influential hit. As soon as the song began climbing the charts during the summer of 1954, a large number of "cover" versions by white performers began to appear. The most successful cover was recorded by a Canadian group, the Crew Cuts. It reached the top ten within a week and largely outsold the Chords' original version. In describing the differences between the Chords' and the Crew Cuts' version of "Sh-Boom," rock scholar Carl Belz noted the following distinctions:

> The Chords' version contains a rich blend between the vocal and instrumental portions of the song. In the Crew Cuts' version, the instrumental background is clearly separated from the lyrics; it is subordinated to the lyrics while they are being sung and it enters only to fill spaces when the lyrics stop. . . . There was the suggestion that the singers were creating lines as they went along and using them to express immediate feelings. . . . These features made the Chords' record distinctive. It projected a fabric of sound in which everything struck the listener at once—instrumental sound, lyrics, fragmentary or improvised lyrics, and all with a powerful incessant beat.

These differences apply to most cover versions of authentic rock 'n' roll records. The story of "Sh-Boom" was repeated many times in 1954 and 1955. An unknown group would record an unknown song on a small independent record label. As soon as one of these records appeared on the popular surveys, it would be covered by a white performer on a major label. A partial list of successful covers from those years includes Fats Domino's "Ain't That a Shame," Little Richard's "Tutti Frutti"—both covered by Pat Boone—the Moonglows' "Sincerely" and the Spaniels' "Goodnight Sweetheart Goodnight"—both covered by the McGuire Sisters—Smiley Lewis's "I Hear You Knockin'"—covered by Gale Storm—and Nappy Brown's "Don't Be Angry"—covered by the Crew Cuts. Although these cover records often outsold the originals, the authentic versions tend to be better known today. As time went by, listeners became accustomed to the sound of authentic rock 'n' roll. They no longer could be satisfied by bland imitations. Although major record companies had more money to promote their cover records, listeners were demanding the real thing. One man who was instrumental in bringing this situation about was Alan Freed. Although his life was filled with controversy, there are few who would deny his importance in ushering in a new musical era.

THE FATHER OF ROCK 'N' ROLL

Alan Freed was the first white disc jockey to play rhythm and blues for the white audience. Freed had an academic background in music and had played trombone in Claude Thornhill's band. He began his radio career by playing classical records on a small station in western Pennsylvania. In 1951, Freed got a classical pro-

Alan Freed takes a break in between shows at the Brooklyn Paramount Theater. (Billy Vera Collection)

gram on a Cleveland station, WJW. Later that year, a local record
store owner named Leo Mintz convinced Freed to follow his classical show with a late-night rock 'n' roll program. A visit to
Mintz's store convinced Freed that a large number of teenagers
were buying and dancing to R&B records. A short time later,
Freed was hosting a new kind of show that he called "The Moondog Rock 'n' Roll House Party."

Freed's show was a tremendous success in Cleveland. Although
he was white, many listeners often took him for a black man.
Freed had a raspy voice and a rapid-fire delivery. He knew how to
use slang and jive talk. His style made him the most innovative
disc jockey in the history of radio. The fact that Freed used the
phrase *rock 'n' roll* to describe familiar R&B material was one of
his greatest contributions. R&B meant music for black people, but
rock 'n' roll meant music for *all* young people. As performers
began to respond to their growing audience, the meaning of *rock
'n' roll* changed. By the mid-fifties, *rock 'n' roll* simply meant
dancing and having a good time. In general, the explicit lyrics of
many R&B records were changing. Many of the new songs were
now geared to the concerns and styles of teenagers. Although this
new music was based on R&B, it had an identity of its own.

In addition to his radio shows, which were now syndicated
around the country, Freed cemented his relationship with the new
music by promoting large concerts. Early in 1952, he promoted a
Moondog Ball at the Cleveland Arena, featuring many top R&B
acts. Some 25,000 teenagers mobbed the 10,000-seat arena. Although the show had to be canceled, the increasing popularity of
this new music could not be denied. The huge crowd consisted
equally of black and white young people, a fact that disturbed
many older citizens of this largely segregated city.

By 1954, Freed had moved to station WINS in New York. Bob
Smith, the station's program director, had been listening to re-
broadcasts of the Moondog show on a small New Jersey station. At
the time of Freed's hiring, WINS had one of the lowest ratings of
all New York stations. Within a year, the station had become the
most popular in the city. Freed was forced to drop the name
Moondog shortly after coming to WINS. The name had been used
for years by a local blind street poet. A local court ruled for the
original Moondog, and Freed was ordered to drop the name by

which millions of listeners knew him. The show was then renamed
"Alan Freed's Rock 'n' Roll Party." At the same time, Freed
adopted a new title—"the king of rock 'n' roll." Whenever Freed
was hosting a concert, his substitute DJ was Paul Sherman. "The
crown prince of rock 'n' roll" (as Sherman was called in those
days), still works for WINS as a news broadcaster. In a recent interview, Sherman described his years as "the prince":

> I really didn't sound anything like Alan, but I was good at
> imitating his style. After the first time I took over for him,
> Freed insisted that I be the only one to replace him. He gave
> me a lot of money for filling in for him, in addition to what the
> station was paying me. It's funny that I was called the "crown
> prince of rock 'n' roll." Before Alan came to the station, I
> never heard much of the music. After a while, I really got to
> like it . . . but Alan—he loved rock 'n' roll. He felt that the
> beat was the main thing. He felt that the "big beat" could
> never be big enough. He used to bang on a phone book over
> the air just to make sure that the beat was heard. He felt that
> this was the main reason that kids got so involved in rock 'n'
> roll.
>
> Although many adults were against the music, I never could
> understand why. I thought that it was good for the kids to
> have their own music. Alan felt this way too. He never en-
> couraged kids to go against their parents, but he believed that
> it was good for young people to be independent. He couldn't
> see anything wrong with teenagers having their own styles and
> their own music. He talked about these things a great deal on
> his show. It's true that he made a lot of money from the busi-
> ness of rock 'n' roll, but he genuinely loved the music.

Freed loved authentic rock 'n' roll so much that he refused to
play any of the well-promoted cover records by white artists. He
also became involved in songwriting. By 1956, he was listed as the
writer or co-writer of a dozen popular rock 'n' roll songs, including
"Maybellene" and "Sincerely." Freed's passion for the new music
made him extremely popular among teenagers and blacks. But he
was widely criticized by many conservative adults. In spite of all
his detractors, Freed's popularity was growing. He appeared in
several movies, including *Don't Knock the Rock* and *Rock Rock*

Rock. More important, his broadcasting style was being copied by DJs all over the country.

As Freed and rock 'n' roll became more successful, a number of newspaper articles were published that were quite hostile to the music and its main promoter. For example, The New York *Daily News* ran a two-part feature that claimed rock 'n' roll caused juvenile delinquency. It accused Freed of being the main wrongdoer. As a result, many churches and school districts banned the music. In the spring of 1958, there was a riot in Boston during one of Freed's many live concerts. For the most part, the young rock 'n' roll audience was enthusiastic, but well-behaved. But when police turned on the house lights in order to get a look at the audience, Freed made a comment. The crowd became upset and unruly. When several violent incidents took place later that day, Freed was blamed. He was arrested and charged with inciting a riot. When the management of WINS failed to stand behind him, Freed quit and moved to WABC. Eventually, all of the charges against him were dropped. By that time, he had spent a fortune in legal fees. Although Freed had made a great deal of money, he declared bankruptcy in July 1959.

Backstage at the Paramount: Singer/trombone player Lillian Briggs rehearses with the band, while Alan Freed (*left*) and Chuck Berry (*wearing hat*) look on. (Billy Vera Collection)

From this point on, Freed's fortunes fell. When the payola scandal rocked the music business in 1960, Freed became one of its most tragic victims. There is little doubt that his vocal support of rock 'n' roll made him an obvious fall guy. He was fired from his job at WABC when he refused to sign a statement that he had never accepted favors in exchange for playing certain records. In 1962, Freed was found guilty on two counts of commercial bribery. He was given a six-month suspended sentence and fined $300. Some two years later, he was found guilty by another grand jury on charges of income tax evasion. By this time, Freed was living in Palm Springs—unemployed, broke, and in poor health. In January 1965, he was admitted to a hospital, suffering from uremia. A short time later, he died. He was only forty-three.

Many people who knew Freed felt that his death was caused by a severe drinking problem. As his personal and financial problems grew, the drinking also increased. But Freed's unhappy ending does not negate his important role in the development of rock 'n' roll. As a disc jockey, he coined a style that suited the excitement of the music. As a promoter, he staged many great live concerts which helped to popularize the music. He was, without a doubt, rock 'n' roll's most important ambassador.

ADULT RESPONSE TO ROCK 'N' ROLL

Many adults felt a great distaste toward rock 'n' roll. In 1955 these adults became more outspoken in their views. They often cited a 1954 report that more than a million young criminals were being arrested each year, and the number was growing. When *Blackboard Jungle,* with its rock 'n' roll sound track, appeared in 1955, it established a permanent link in the minds of adults between teenage music and juvenile delinquency. The following description in the *Britannica Book of the Year* for 1956 expressed the way many adults viewed rock 'n' roll:

> The rowdy element (in the popular music of 1955) was represented by "Rock Around the Clock," theme song of the con-

Bill Haley in 1958 (*left*) and at a revival concert in 1973 (Billy Vera Collection)

troversial film *Blackboard Jungle.* The rock 'n' roll school in general concentrated on a minimum of melodic line and a maximum of rhythmic noise, deliberately competing with the jungle itself.

There is very little actual evidence that the music inspired young people to become violent. Many adults, however, were so upset about rock 'n' roll that they became violent. Some preached an aggressive stand toward the music.

The enormous popularity of Elvis Presley caused an even more negative attitude toward rock 'n' roll by many of its critics. The appearance of a white man shaking his hips, gyrating his pelvis, and singing like a black man was more than certain members of the older generation could take. At times, their reactions were quite drastic. Actions included bans, arrests, and physical destruction in their protests of rock 'n' roll. A Buffalo, New York, disc jockey was fired for playing Elvis's records. Another DJ in Chicago smashed Presley records on the air. One used-car dealer in Cincinnati guaranteed to break fifty of "The Pelvis's" records with each purchase. It was clear that many of rock 'n' roll's more outspoken critics were out to get Presley. Rock 'n' roll had to be stopped before all of America's children were corrupted.

There can be little doubt that many of rock 'n' roll's most vocal critics feared the growing influence of black culture upon American life. This attitude created several shameful and needless incidents. One of the most notorious involved Nat King Cole, a black singer who was not even remotely connected with rock 'n' roll. While Cole was performing before a white audience in Birmingham, Alabama, in 1956, five white men leaped on the stage and began to beat him up. Fortunately, police quickly subdued the attackers and Cole was not hurt. One of the men arrested was identified as a leader of the White Citizens' Council, a racist group that promoted a boycott of Negro music, bop, and rock 'n' roll.

In 1956, rock 'n' roll seemed to take off. Teenagers accounted for half of all record sales, and many of the records they bought were by black artists. These included "I'm in Love Again," Fats Domino; "Roll Over Beethoven," Chuck Berry; "Treasure of Love," Clyde McPhatter; and "Since I Met You Baby," Ivory Joe Hunter. For the first time, these artists were regularly outselling their white imitators. Aware of an expanding market, some R&B performers began modifying their words and music in order to sell to the larger white audience. Many of the records made by these artists are among the greatest in the history of rock 'n' roll.

But the most important musical event of 1956 was the phenomenal success of a twenty-one-year-old truck driver from Memphis, Tennessee.

Many rock historians feel that if Elvis Presley had not come along exactly when he did, it might have been necessary to invent him. Although many fine black performers were crossing over to the pop charts, there were record companies that were still hostile toward this music. In addition, white teenagers did not have a real idol. Bill Haley's music was popular, but his sound and looks were not the stuff that idols are made of.

A Memphis singer named Carl Perkins had a hit in 1956 with "Blue Suede Shoes." The song was in a style similar to Elvis's. It expressed the teenage outlook as well as any song in early rock 'n' roll. Perkins was a talented musician and songwriter, but he was not destined to become a superstar. In fact, when Elvis recorded "Blue Suede Shoes" on his first album, in 1956, listeners seemed to forget about Perkins. That year belonged to one man—Elvis Presley.

ELVIS PRESLEY—"THE PELVIS"

Elvis Presley was the most important artist in the early development of rock 'n' roll. He combined a unique singing style with tough good looks and sexy gyrations. He appealed to teenagers of both sexes. Elvis's popularity was unmatched during the early years of rock 'n' roll. It has been surpassed only once in the history of rock—by the Beatles. Elvis was the first rock 'n' roll artist to have a series of million-selling singles—eighteen between 1956 and 1960. He was also the first to establish and maintain an independent career in movies. Within a short time after his explosion onto the scene, Elvis had managed to win over not only the kids but their parents too. By that time, however, he had softened his style considerably. The hits that made Elvis a great rock 'n' roll artist were recorded mostly in 1956. He also recorded ten sides during 1954 and 1955 on the Sun label in Memphis. Although none of these records made the pop charts, many rock 'n' roll purists consider them his best work. On some of these early sides,

Elvis Presley with fans (Billy Vera Collection)

Elvis sang in a style that had previously been used only by black performers. His work at Sun and at RCA in 1956 represented the most important turning point in the history of rock 'n' roll.

Elvis had five of the top twenty records in 1956. His first release for RCA, "Heartbreak Hotel," quickly took the top position in the pop and country charts, as well as making the top five on most R&B surveys. At one point, he became the first artist to have the number one and two records at the same time. More remarkably, these two songs—"Hound Dog" and "Don't Be Cruel"—were the A and B sides of the same record. A little later in the year, Elvis's first ballad, "Love Me Tender," sold over 800,000 copies in advance orders before its release. His record sales were so phenomenal that RCA had to rent record pressing facilities from its competitors to meet the demand. The music business had never known a performer to achieve such immediate and overwhelming success. Nor had anyone ever seen such a huge number of near-hysterical young fans like those Elvis attracted. The King of rock 'n' roll had arrived.

THE LATE FIFTIES—1957–59

By the late fifties, many adults began reaching a truce with rock 'n' roll. Record companies and radio stations looked for entertainers and songs that would appeal to teens without offending adults. New performers came from many sources. A few of these new singers were authentic rock 'n' roll talents—Buddy Holly and the Everly Brothers, for example. Many record companies looked for singers with abilities similar to Elvis's. Capitol Records launched a search for such a performer and came up with Gene Vincent and his hit record, "Be-Bop-a-Lula." Other companies and producers settled for young men who simply looked like Elvis. One such performer was Fabian, an amateur from Philadelphia. Although his musical talents were below average, he had two big hits, "Turn Me Loose" and "Tiger." Movies and television provided performers with built-in followings. These included Tab Hunter, Sal Mineo, and Ricky Nelson. Still another way of creating new rock 'n' roll singers was to take a popular crooner or a country singer

Gene Vincent and his Blue Caps (Billy Vera Collection)

and record him singing a rock 'n' roll song. Although the new rock 'n' roll performers varied greatly in background and talent, they all shared a relatively innocent teen outlook that was more acceptable to adults than the explicit sexuality of some rhythm and blues songs.

The lyrics of the new teen tunes were concerned with topics like going to a dance ("At the Hop," "White Sport Coat," "Short Fat Fanny"); resenting school ("School Days"), declaring teenage love ("Peggy Sue," "Party Doll"); and fearing criticism or punishment from parents ("Teenage Crush," "Young Love," "Wake up Little Susie"). These songs catered to the unique needs and experiences of teenagers. The attitudes conveyed in these songs of the late fifties provided much of the basis for the fifties revival in the seventies.

One of the most important events of 1957 was the introduction of a local Philadelphia TV show to national audiences. "American Bandstand" showcased teenage music, dances, and styles. The viewer at home felt like a participant. In a sense, "Bandstand" was a symbol of victory for teenagers: the program belonged to them. At its peak, the show was broadcast every day after school for ninety minutes. It was broadcast over 100 stations and reached no less than 20 million teenagers.

"American Bandstand" launched its host Dick Clark to fame and fortune. Clark was clean-cut, and his suave manner and winning smile reassured parents that rock 'n' roll might not be so bad. Clark insisted on a strict code of behavior and dress on the show. The camera often switched from the dancers to shots of Clark overseeing the proceedings. He was like a young schoolteacher supervising his students.

By 1958, Clark was one of the most important people in the music business. He owned large percentages of several Philadelphia-based record and publishing companies and had the power to create hits and new dance trends. When Congress investigated the widespread practice of playing records in return for money or favors, Clark was singled out by one congressman as the "top dog in the payola scandal." Although the "play for pay" revelations ruined the careers of Alan Freed and many other disc jockeys, Clark escaped almost untouched.

Many rock 'n' roll historians consider the late fifties and early

Dick Clark presenting a gold record to teen idol Jimmy Clanton on "American Bandstand" (Neal Hollander Collection)

sixties a boring and dormant period for the music. Many radio stations, in an attempt to counteract payola, switched from shows that featured personality disc jockeys to top forty programming. Records were played on the basis of singles sales alone. This procedure tended to reflect the taste of the younger singles buyers. Album purchasers, who tended to be somewhat older and more developed in their musical taste, found their preferences ignored by top forty programmers. The records that got played did not really represent what most listeners wanted to hear.

Another important sign of the decline of rock 'n' roll at this time was the disappearance of many of its greatest stars from the music scene. Elvis went into the army and came out a pop singer, Little Richard quit performing to become a minister, Jerry Lee Lewis married his thirteen-year-old cousin and was effectively banned from the music business. A plane crash in February 1959 killed Buddy Holly, Richie Valens, and the Big Bopper. Many of the youngsters who grew up with rock 'n' roll felt that an era was ending. In spite of this, however, there were a number of good records during the closing year of the decade.

In 1959, Ray Charles combined gospel music with the blues and had a gigantic hit with "What'd I Say." The song was widely covered and became the year's most influential hit. Two other gospel-influenced records also created a lot of excitement in 1959— "Shout" by the Isley Brothers and "Lonely Teardrops" by Jackie Wilson. These three songs helped the widespread acceptance of soul music in both the R&B and pop markets. Soul music seemed to be drawn more from the gospel-blues tradition than most rock 'n' roll.

During this time, other kinds of black music were becoming popular. Bobby Robinson, an independent record producer, heard Wilbert Harrison do a conventional blues shuffle in a small club called Kansas City. Although this type of song rarely was found on the pop charts, Harrison's record became a big hit. Nina Simone, an ex-piano teacher from North Carolina, had a hit with the ballad "I Loves You Porgy." The record was much closer to jazz than to pop or R&B. A jazz hit was even rarer than a blues shuffle. Nevertheless, Nina Simone did quite well with "Porgy" in 1959. It appeared as though the sixties would witness the increasing popularity of many black artists and their music.

THE EARLY SIXTIES

One of the most important trends of the early sixties was the national dance crazes. Before "American Bandstand" and other national television dance programs, there were many local styles of dancing. Because these shows were so popular, the trend spread quickly around the country. If a dance became popular on "Bandstand," it was picked up by kids in all areas. Performers tried to become identified with a particular dance. Chubby Checker, for example, performed and danced the Twist on "Bandstand," and soon the dance became tremendously popular. Although Hank

1956—Chubby Checker—1973 (Billy Vera Collection)

Ballard wrote and recorded the original version of "The Twist," Checker's appearances on "Bandstand" linked him with the song. Eventually, the Twist became an international rage among adults as well as teenagers. Although the beat was identical to that of many previous R&B records, the dance was hailed as a new phenomenon.

The widespread success of the Twist seemed to indicate a growing demand for records with a rock 'n' roll beat. A number of new records appeared with familiar rhythms and new dance names. Record labels did their best to get a particular artist associated with a new dance craze. Cameo-Parkway Records of Philadelphia, with its close connection to "American Bandstand," was behind many of these. The label had already made a lot of money with Chubby Checker's "The Twist," "Let's Twist Again," and "Slow Twistin'." Checker's success on the label was followed by Dee Dee Sharp's "Mashed Potato Time"; The Dovells' "The Bristol Stomp"; the Orlons' "Wah Watusi"; and a number of others.

Most of the dance hits of the early sixties stressed the catchy beat and featured lyrics that described the steps. These records were often enjoyable to hear, although they contained little genuine emotion. At the same time, there seemed to be a renewed interest in slow songs that featured singers with the gentle mood and emotional sound of some earlier records. Several popular records of this type during the early sixties were "Daddy's Home," Shep and the Limelights, and "Those Oldies but Goodies," Little Caesar and the Romans. Record companies began releasing collections of songs from the group era (1954–1958). The fifties were hardly over, and already the first wave of nostalgia had begun.

There were many important innovations in recording which came about during the early sixties. Producers were becoming ever more skillful in combining traditional musical forms with these new recording techniques. These advancements enabled creative producers to develop new moods and emotions in their records. The Motown organization, owned by Berry Gordy, was a company that used these new techniques with great success. The records produced under Gordy's supervision combined the blues-gospel feel with sophisticated musical arrangements and advanced recording techniques. By the mid-sixties, Gordy had put together a spectacular roster of talented performers, including Smokey Robinson and the Miracles, Marvin Gaye, the Supremes, Martha and the Vandellas, the Marvellettes, Mary Wells, the Tempations, the Four Tops, Junior Walker and the All Stars, and child prodigy Stevie Wonder. Beginning in the early sixties, these artists made some of the best and most popular records of the decade.

Little Caesar and the Romans ("Bleecker" Bob Plotnik Collection)

Smokey Robinson and the Miracles ("Bleecker" Bob Plotnik Collection)

One of the most important new sounds to develop at Motown and elsewhere came from the many female groups to have hits at that time. During the fifties, women were used mainly to back up male singers. Surpisingly, there had only been four hit records by black female groups before 1959: "Eddie My Love," the Teen Queens (1956); "Mr. Lee," the Bobettes (1957); "Down the Aisle of Love," the Quintones (1958); and "Maybe," the Chantels (1958). By the early sixties, however, a new feminine sound had become extremely popular.

The first "girl-group" to have a string of hits in the sixties was the Shirelles. These included, "Dedicated to the One I Love" and "Soldier Boy." Motown pitched in with hits by the Marvellettes and Martha and the Vandellas. The most successful female group from Motown was the Supremes, but they did not develop their popular sound until 1964.

Some of the better records of the girl-group era were produced

The Teen Queens (Billy
Vera Collection)

by a young producer named Phil Spector. His records during this
period were both innovative and popular. Spector developed a
sound that contained lush orchestrations, and a snappy rhythm
which was often provided by tambourines and hand clapping.
These techniques added drama to his productions. Spector's girl-

The Shirelles—the most successful "girl group" of early rock 'n' roll
("Bleecker" Bob Plotnik Collection)

group hits included "He's a Rebel" by the Crystals and "Be My Baby" by the Ronettes. He is probably the only producer in the history of the music business to become better known than most of his artists. As writer Nik Cohn recalls, "His records were the loudest, fiercest, most magnificent explosions that rock had yet produced or dreamed of."

THE NEW ROCK SCENE

The widespread changes of the mid-sixties were reflected in the revolution that took place in popular music. While black artists were becoming more dominated by their producers, a new breed of white singer-songwriters was beginning to make its presence felt. Important names to emerge during this era were Bob Dylan, Paul Simon, the Beatles, and the Rolling Stones. Simon and Dylan, at this time, were mostly using traditional folk and folk-blues forms to express their highly sophisticated ideas. The Beatles and the Rolling Stones, on the other hand, were self-contained groups that played traditional rock 'n' roll in addition to their own material. Both groups paid particular tribute to Chuck Berry by recording many of his songs. The Beatles also included songs by Carl Perkins, Little Richard, and Smokey Robinson in their repertoire. As they progressed, both groups became much more sophisticated in their lyrics. Nevertheless, much of the new rock music was based on traditional blues and authentic rock 'n' roll.

During the sixties, a large number of young people seemed to become more aware of themselves and the conditions around them. Some became involved in antiwar and civil rights activities. Others experimented with drugs, eastern religions, and other mind-altering activities. Many musicians and songwriters echoed these concerns in their work. By the end of the decade, several new trends had become influential. These included art-rock, protest music, and psychedelic music. Each one of these forms would require more elaboration than the scope of this book permits. But collectively, they took popular music to extremes that the early rock 'n' rollers never could have imagined.

Poets like Dylan and Simon brought rock to new lyrical heights.

Innovators like the Beatles broke new musical ground, and electronic wizards like Jimi Hendrix were threatening to bust the sound barrier. At the same time, however, rock had become respectable. Conductor Leonard Bernstein appeared on TV during the late sixties and declared that he liked much of the new rock. Established crooners, who hated rock 'n' roll during the fifties, were now looking for suitable rock songs to record.

By the seventies, many observers felt that rock had run its course. Jazz had found its way into R&B, and the result was fusion music and disco. Performers like KISS and Alice Cooper began to turn to extreme theatrical devices and costumes to get their music across. Many observers feel that these trends indicate a stagnant period for rock music. It is not difficult to understand why many listeners have turned their attention to the more basic sounds of early rock 'n' roll.

A writer for a New York newspaper recently compared the early rock 'n' roll years to the pioneering days of the Old West. Just as western movies and TV shows provide a glimpse into this exciting stage in our history, rock 'n' roll takes us back to another crucial period. The fifties witnessed the coming together of black and white musical traditions that had for years been separated. The mixture of white country music and black blues had been developing for years. But in the fifties, the explosion took place, and rock 'n' roll was born.

As we will see, rock 'n' roll developed in several geographic areas at the same time. Young people were ready for something new, and the big beat was that something. Within a few years, the sound spread all over the world. Rock 'n' roll became the international language of young people. To understand this language, listen to some of the great old rock 'n' roll records. Many of them sound just as good today as they did back in the fifties.

Authentic Rock 'n' Roll Styles and Performers

3

Rock 'n' Roll Styles

The combinations of musical styles which evolved in certain key areas of the United States led to the development of five distinct types of rock 'n' roll between 1954 and 1956. As defined by rock scholar Charlie Gillett in his book *The Sound of the City,* these five rock 'n' roll styles were: northern band music, New Orleans rock 'n' roll, rockabilly, Chicago style rock 'n' roll, and vocal group music. All five styles used dance rhythms that came from rhythm and blues, and all expressed both the traditions and changing attitudes of the particular local audiences.

Since each style had a particular local flavor, the new music appealed to people with similar backgrounds and experiences. While traditional popular music tried to attract a mass audience regardless of age or location, rock 'n' roll was geared to young people in particular areas of the country. There was overlapping between the styles, although each retained a good deal of its particular character. As the various forms became nationally popular, teenagers in different parts of the country began to recognize a common language in both the lyrics and the beat of certain records. By the late fifties and early sixties, two new styles became popular—gospel-influenced rock 'n' roll and music by female vocal groups.

NORTHERN BAND MUSIC:
BILL HALEY AND THE COMETS

The music of Bill Haley and the Comets is the foremost example of the northern band style of rock 'n' roll. This music combined country, dixieland, and dance-band rhythm and blues. This style of R&B, best exemplified by bands like Louis Jordan's, attempted to create excitement with musicians playing solos on their backs and climbing on their instruments. Another characteristic of these bands was chorus singing by the musicians. The Comets borrowed many of these devices. Saxophone player Rudy Pompelli, who is the only original Comet still working with Haley, took solos consisting of one or two notes while lying on his back. The band often sang the choruses of songs in unison, and successfully created a happy and fun-loving feeling.

Bill Haley was born in Highland Park, Michigan, in 1927. Bill came from a musical family. His father was a country banjo picker and his mother played the organ at the local church. Both parents encouraged Bill to study the guitar. At fifteen, he went on the road with a band called the Down Homers. Later on, Bill started his own country and western combo, the Saddlemen. It is worth mentioning that not many singers from northern cities became country and western performers. Haley had traveled around the South and was moved by the music of Hank Williams. He was hoping to achieve fame as a yodeler, but also had a strong interest in the blues.

Bill considered leaving show business in the early fifties, but he landed a job at a small radio station in Chester, Pennsylvania. Aside from playing a daily live show with his group, Bill doubled as the station's sports announcer. While his work on the radio station did not bring in a lot of money, it did bring Haley in contact with a large variety of records by black bands such as Louis Jordan, Lucky Millinder, and Lionel Hampton. Haley began thinking about combining country and western with black big band music and placing this combination inside a rhythm and blues beat.

By the early fifties, Haley became aware of an ever-widening gap between the tastes of young people and the preferences of pop

Bill Haley and the Comets (Courtesy of Columbia Pictures)

radio programmers. He began to experiment with the various styles that impressed him. Haley took the music of the big bands and adapted the lines for his small, guitar-dominated group. He also moved the rhythmic accent from the first and third to the second and fourth beats of each four-beat musical measure. Haley believed that this change in rhythmic accent would better suit the changing tastes of dancers and listeners.

Bill Haley and the Comets began to record this new music in the early fifties. Their first hit record on the Essex label was "Crazy Man Crazy" in 1953. The group became sufficiently well known to attract a contract from a major label, Decca Records. In 1954, the group had several hits, including "Shake Rattle and Roll" and "Dim Dim the Lights." "Shake Rattle and Roll" had been written and previously recorded by a rhythm and blues artist named Joe Turner. Haley reworked Turner's explicitly sexual lyrics and speeded up the slow, suggestive beat of the original. The record was being directed at the emerging teenage market. Although his vocals always had a country twang, some of his records made it on the R&B charts.

Nineteen fifty-five belonged to Bill Haley and his Comets. The success of the movie *Blackboard Jungle* sent its theme song, "Rock

Around the Clock" to the top of the charts. Although the record had been a moderate hit for the group in 1954, "Rock Around the Clock" took on a new importance that went beyond its huge sales figures (over 17 million records sold). It was the first rock 'n' roll song to reach the top of the charts in England. The song became the theme of the teenage revolution. Several riots that attended showings of *Blackboard Jungle* gave the false impression that "Rock Around the Clock" was a call to rebellion. In truth, the song was simply a lively dance shuffle whose lyrics spoke of dancing until dawn and having a good time.

The group appeared in a number of movies after 1955. The most famous of these was *Rock Around the Clock* and *Don't Knock the Rock.* There were several follow-up records which sold well for the group, particularly a cover version of Bobby Charles's "See You Later Alligator." In 1956, however, record sales tailed off quite a bit.

Bill Haley lacked the sex appeal of an Elvis and the wildness of a Jerry Lee Lewis. He seemed more like a pudgy, fun-loving country boy whose trademark was a spit-curl that ran down the middle of his forehead. His music captured the beat and the lingo of rock 'n' roll. His lyrics did not penetrate like Chuck Berry's; his music did not excite like Little Richard's. But in 1955, Bill Haley was the right man with the right song.

During the early sixties, Bill and the group worked regularly abroad, though they were not in great demand in the United States. In 1967, Bill began to recognize a great renewal of interest in his music in London, Paris, Amsterdam, and other major European cities. In 1969, Haley worked at the rock 'n' roll revival concert at Madison Square Garden in New York. Since that time, he has been a star on the oldies circuit. He co-starred in the 1973 film, *Let the Good Times Roll* with Little Richard and Fats Domino. Bill Haley and his Comets are currently working at concert halls both here and abroad.

For the most part, the northern band style of rock 'n' roll began and ended with Haley. The other styles enjoyed a much longer period of success. Although the music and style of the Comets were widely imitated by hopeful bands in northern cities, there were few successful records in this style by other groups.

BILL HALEY AND HIS COMETS
COLLECTORS' GUIDE
—Smash hit in that category

Date	Song	Label	Pop	R&B	C&W
5/53	Crazy Man Crazy	Essex	*		
8/54	Shake Rattle and Roll	Decca	*		
11/54	Dim Dim the Lights	Decca	*	*	
2/55	Mambo Rock	Decca	*		
3/55	Birth of the Boogie	Decca			
5/55	Rock Around the Clock	Decca	*	*	*
7/55	Razzle-Dazzle/Two Hound Dogs	Decca	*		
11/55	Burn That Candle	Decca	*		
12/55	See You Later Alligator	Decca	*	*	*
3/56	R-O-C-K	Decca			
3/56	The Saints Rock 'n' Roll	Decca			
5/56	Hot Dog Buddy Buddy	Decca			
7/56	Rip It Up	Decca			
10/56	Rudy's Rock	Decca			
3/57	Forty Cups of Coffee	Decca			
6/57	Billy Goat	Decca			
3/58	Skinny Minnie	Decca			
10/59	Joey's Song	Decca			
1/60	Skokian	Decca			

ALBUMS

Date	Album	Label
1/56	*Rock Around the Clock*	Decca

NEW ORLEANS ROCK 'N' ROLL

New Orleans has served as one of the most important melting pots of American music. Founded by the French in 1718, the city later became Spanish property, before being returned to France. In 1803, New Orleans finally joined the United States as part of the Louisiana Purchase. This convenient seaport became a wealthy center of commerce in the years before the Civil War. The city also developed a reputation as a place where a good time was easily had. People from many cultures were attracted to the diverse pleasures of New Orleans. From an exotic mixture of French, Spanish, English, African, Creole, and Cajun peoples came a culture, language, and entertainment that was unique for an American city.

Various musical traditions which have made themselves felt in both jazz and rock 'n' roll sprang from this atmosphere—the rolling boogie-woogie styles of the barrelhouse piano players, the ensemble horn styles of black funeral bands, the raw country blues singers from the nearby Mississippi Delta, and the improvisations of the many local jazz bands. Many of these elements can be heard in most New Orleans rock 'n' roll.

One of the most important influences on New Orleans rock 'n' roll was the work of a rhythm and blues piano player known as Professor Longhair. Although he only had one national R&B hit ("Bald Head" in 1955), his strong shuffle piano feel influenced a generation of New Orleans keyboard players. Roy Byrd was one of the first performers to assume a bizarre name. Calling his group Professor Longhair and His Shuffling Hungarians, Byrd had a talent for humorous novelty songs that served as a model for successful New Orleans performers like Huey "Piano" Smith and the Clowns. Although he never reached the rock 'n' roll audience, he was one of the first to develop and record New Orleans rock 'n' roll.

One of the essential features of the New Orleans sound is a rolling bass figure, which is embraced by the rhythm section and horns. This characteristic, which dates back to Longhair's early records, provides the music with a deep, rich low end sound. The high end of the music is handled by rolling boogie-woogie style piano fills. In between these two extremes, one usually finds a strong male rhythm and blues voice or the warm sound of a tenor sax. In contrast to the other styles, New Orleans rock 'n' roll records use few guitar solos. Excitement is created by the tension between the singer or sax player's performance and the full, chugging riffs of the band.

Two relatively unknown people who were vital in the development of the New Orleans style were bandleader songwriter Dave Bartholomew and recording engineer Cosimo Matassa. Bartholomew was the producer of many of the New Orleans hits. Originally a jazz trumpet player, Bartholomew organized the band that played on most of the important New Orleans recording sessions. This group of musicians played in a manner that was extremely tight (together), yet relaxed. Bartholomew was also one of the most successful writers of the fifties, co-writing all of Domino's hits.

All of the important New Orleans records were made at the J&M studio. Cosimo Matassa, owner and chief engineer of J&M, perfected the rich sound-quality which still holds up admirably. Matassa's recording techniques were simple—turn on the machine and capture the natural sound of the music without using any electronic tricks. Twenty-five years later, engineers and musicians try in vain to achieve this rich and authentic sound.

The first R&B hit in the New Orleans style was "The Fat Man," recorded in 1949 by Fats Domino. Although he continued to have success from that point on, other New Orleans performers were not so lucky in the early fifties. Smiley Lewis, for example, made several memorable records, but had little commercial success. Aside from "The Bells Are Ringing," which was a minor R&B hit in 1952, and Gale Storm's million-selling cover of "I Hear You Knockin'," Smiley never did attract a substantial following.

Aside from Fats Domino, the first singer to have a hit in the New Orleans style was Lloyd Price with "Lawdy Miss Clawdy" in 1952. The record was produced in typical New Orleans style. While Price sang in a voice that was both rich and raspy, the band laid down a strong accompaniment that included the rolling piano of Fats Domino. "Lawdy Miss Clawdy" was a big hit and was one of the first R&B records to attract a large number of white sales. Price made several good records in the early fifties, but was unable to duplicate his initial success. In the late fifties, Price had a series of hits on the ABC label: "Just Because," "Stagger Lee," and "Personality" were all recorded in a slick version of the New Orleans style that sold well in the pop market.

Another memorable New Orleans style record on the Specialty label was "The Things I Used to Do," by Guitar Slim. In one of the most exceptional recording sessions to date, the raw blues singing and virtuoso electric guitar playing of Guitar Slim were combined with the gospel-blues arranging of Ray Charles. The record was a landmark in the history of rhythm and blues. It sold a million

Lloyd Price (Neal
Hollander Collection)

copies and is among the most creative music to come out of J&M studios.

Nineteen fifty-five was the year that the New Orleans sound made itself felt on the pop hit parade. The first singer to have hits in this style was a white ballad singer who sang in a Bing Crosby–type of baritone. Pat Boone, like other Americans, considered rhythm and blues unrefined. When Randy Wood, president of Dot records, suggested that Boone cover songs like Fats Domino's "Ain't That a Shame," and Little Richard's, "Tutti Frutti," he was surprised indeed. But Wood, who operated a successful mail order record business, knew that southern white teenagers were buying R&B records in increasing numbers. Wood simply copied the New Orleans style arrangements of Fats Domino and Little Richard and cloned Boone's voice onto them.

Although Boone's cover records outsold the originals, they may have helped create interest in the authentic performances. By the end of 1956, Domino and Little Richard were making the pop charts, while Boone was able to return to the kind of ballads that he was more comfortable with.

Fats Domino and Little Richard were the first authentic performers to have pop hits in the New Orleans style of rock 'n' roll. Domino, who became the only successful R&B performer to have a large number of pop hits, had been the most important figure in the style since 1949. Little Richard did not live or record in New Orleans, and his frantic singing style was in sharp contrast to Domino's good-humored approach. Nevertheless, both men often used the same musicians and arrangers on their records. In general, Richard's records were much more intense and were performed at a faster tempo than those of Fats. While Little Richard probably influenced a wider range of rock 'n' roll singers, Fats served as a model for most of the performers who recorded in the New Orleans style.

Many of the New Orleans rock 'n' roll hits of the fifties and early sixties were humorous novelty records. Some of the more popular records in this style were made by Shirley and Lee ("Let the Good Times Roll") and Huey "Piano" Smith and the Clowns ("Rockin' Pneumonia," "Don't You Just Know It"). In 1959, Frankie Ford, a protégé of Smith's, had a big hit with "Sea Cruise." All of these records were strongly influenced in their moods and arrangements by Fats Domino.

Shirley and Lee—"The Sweethearts of the Blues" ("Bleecker" Bob Plotnik Collection)

The New Orleans style continued to be a major influence in the early sixties, although the popularity of both Domino and Little Richard decreased considerably. The central figure in this style was now a songwriter, pianist, and arranger named Allen Toussaint. Showing a strong leaning toward Ray Charles's gospel-style piano, Toussaint produced records by Ernie K. Doe, Clarence "Frogman" Henry, Aaron Neville, and many others. One of the few New Orleans artists to have non-Toussaint hits was Chris Kenner ("I Like It Like That," "Land of the Thousand Dances").

For the most part, the New Orleans sound was recorded locally. Bobby Robinson, owner of New York–based Fire/Fury Records, was the only producer from outside New Orleans to have regular productions in that city. His biggest hit in this style was "Ya Ya" by Lee Dorsey. The song featured a Toussaint-inspired up-tempo arrangement and good natured, humorous lyrics that were typical of the New Orleans style.

Sitting here la-la, waiting for my ya-ya, uh huh, uh-huh,
Sitting here la-la, waiting for my ya-ya, uh huh, uh-huh,
It may sound funny, but I don't believe she's comin', uh-huh.

Yeah baby hurry, don't leave me worried, uh huh, uh-huh,
Yeah baby hurry, don't leave me worried, uh huh, uh-huh.
You know how I love you oh how I love you, uh-huh, uh-huh.

Robinson also had hits with Buster Brown ("Fannie Mae") and
Bobby Marchan ("Something's on Your Mind") in the early sixties.
Marchan had been the lead singer on Huey Smith and the Clowns'
two hits, although many people thought the voice they were hearing belonged to Smith.

In the seventies, New Orleans rock 'n' roll is still dominated by
the work of Allen Toussaint. His productions with the group La-
belle resulted in several big hits in the mid-seventies. He also produced a Lee Dorsey album in 1978 that was well received.
Contemporary rock performers like Dr. John and The Band have
incorporated the New Orleans sound in their songs. The rolling
boogie-woogie style of piano playing and rhythmic horn arrangements have become absorbed in the vocabulary of popular music.

NEW ORLEANS COLLECTORS' GUIDE

Year	Song	Artist	Label
1950	Bald Head	Roy Byrd (Prof. Longhair)	Mercury
1952	The Bells Are Ringing	Smiley Lewis	Imperial
1958	Don't You Just Know It	Huey "Piano" Smith and the Clowns	Ace
1956	I Feel Good	Shirley and Lee	Aladdin
1952	Lawdy Miss Clawdy	Lloyd Price	Specialty
1952	Ooh Ooh Oow/Restless Heart	Lloyd Price	Specialty
1952	I'm Gone	Shirley and Lee	Aladdin
1957	Rockin' Pneumonia and The Boogie Woogie Flu	Huey "Piano" Smith and the Clowns	Ace
1959	Sea Cruise	Frankie Ford	Ace
1958	Walkin' with Mr. Lee	Lee Allen and His Band	Ember

FATS DOMINO

Fats Domino's high-pitched nasal voice and unique "Cajun" accent immediately identified his records. His first one, "The Fat Man," was a big rhythm and blues hit in 1950. It presented a good humored autobiography of its performer and showed him to be a proficient pianist as well as a confident singer. As his records began edging over into the pop market, his voice deepened somewhat and lost some of its rough edge. His records coupled a plaintive, yet childlike, singing style with a catchy beat. Most of Fats' songs were less raw and sexually explicit than most other blues-based singers. He was, therefore, more acceptable to the pop audience. Domino was the only successful rhythm and blues singer to have consistent popularity in the pop charts without greatly changing his style.

Antoine Domino was born in New Orleans in 1928, one of nine children. He began playing the piano at an early age. After working on an ice truck for several years, Fats took on another job, which almost ended his piano-playing career. While he was working in a factory that manufactured bedsprings, Fats' hand was badly gashed by a heavy spring that fell on it. Several stitches were required, and it was thought that he might not be able to move the hand again. Through exercise and determination, he reacquired almost full use of the hand and was able to continue with his piano playing.

In 1949, during an engagement at the Hideaway Club in New Orleans, Al Chuld and Dave Bartholomew of Imperial Records came to hear Fats. The result was an immediate record contract. Shortly thereafter, Fats and Dave Bartholomew co-wrote "The Fat Man." Bartholomew, a former trumpet player with the Duke Ellington Band, was the producer and arranger on all of Domino's hits. While Fats played his full-chord boogie-woogie piano style, the band played riffs which stressed the dance beat. The records were of two types—fast exuberant shuffles and slow ballads with a strong triplet feel. About three-quarters of the way through most of Fats' records, there is a tenor sax solo by Lee Allen or Herb

Fats Domino (Neal Hollander Collection)

Hardesty. The tone of the saxophone usually matched the controlled and melodic quality of Domino's singing.

Fats had a number of rhythm and blues hits in the early fifties after "The Fat Man," but he did not cross over until 1956. Beginning with the up-tempo shuffle, "I'm in Love Again," Domino was rarely without a chart record for the next five years. The ideas for many of his songs came from everyday expressions like, "Be My Guest," "I'm Ready," and "Ain't That a Shame." Fats also found great success recording standards in his unique style, and he had hits with remakes of "Blueberry Hill," "My Blue Heaven," and "When My Dreamboat Comes Home."

Although Fats never had a number one hit, his popularity was amazingly consistent. His records were, for the most part, simple, danceable, and memorable. They contained a quality which is difficult to describe. Although there were other good records in a similar style, the public could not find a replacement for Fats' childlike voice or the strong beat of Bartholemew's arrangements.

In the late sixties, Fats moved to Warner Brothers Records and had a moderate hit with his version of the Beatles' "Lady Madonna." Today Fats still lives in his native New Orleans with his wife and eight children. He appeared in the movie *Let the Good Times Roll* and can still be seen in clubs and concerts throughout the country.

FATS DOMINO COLLECTORS' GUIDE
°—Smash hit in that category

Date	Song	Label	Pop	R&B	C&W
3/50	The Fat Man	Imperial		°	
12/50	Every Night About This Time	Imperial		°	
12/51	Rockin' Chair	Imperial		°	
5/52	Goin' Home	Imperial		°	
12/52	How Long	Imperial		°	
4/53	Goin' to the River	Imperial		°	
7/53	Please Don't Leave Me	Imperial		°	
10/53	Rose Mary	Imperial		°	
12/53	Something's Wrong	Imperial		°	
3/54	You Done Me Wrong	Imperial		°	
3/55	Don't You Know	Imperial		°	
7/55	Ain't That a Shame	Imperial	°	°	
9/55	All By Myself	Imperial		°	
11/55	Poor Me	Imperial		°	
2/56	Bo Weevil/Don't Blame It on Me	Imperial		°	
4/56	I'm in Love Again/My Blue Heaven	Imperial	°	°	
7/56	When My Dreamboat Comes Home/So Long	Imperial		°	
9/56	Blueberry Hill	Imperial	°	°	
12/56	Blue Monday	Imperial	°	°	
1/57	What's the Reason I'm Not Pleasing You	Imperial			
2/57	I'm Walkin'	Imperial		°	
5/57	Valley of Tears	Imperial	°	°	
5/57	It's You I Love	Imperial	°		
8/57	When I See You	Imperial			
8/57	What Will I Tell My Heart	Imperial			
10/57	I Still Love You	Imperial			
10/57	Wait and See	Imperial		°	
12/57	The Big Beat	Imperial			
12/57	I Want You to Know	Imperial			
3/58	Yes, My Darling	Imperial			
4/58	Sick and Tired/No No	Imperial		°	
6/58	Little Mary	Imperial		°	
9/58	Young School Girl	Imperial			
11/58	Whole Lotta Loving	Imperial	°	°	
1/59	Coquette	Imperial			
2/59	Telling Lies	Imperial		°	
2/59	When the Saints Go Marching In	Imperial			

Date	Song	Label	Pop	R&B	C&W
5/59	I'm Ready	Imperial	°	°	
5/59	Margie	Imperial			
8/59	I Want to Walk You Home	Imperial	°	°	
8/59	I'm Gonna Be a Wheel Some Day	Imperial	°		
11/59	Be My Guest	Imperial	°	°	
11/59	I've Been Around	Imperial		°	
2/60	Country Boy	Imperial			
2/60	If You Need Me	Imperial			
5/60	Tell Me That You Love Me	Imperial			
5/60	Before I Grow Too Old	Imperial			
6/60	Walking to New Orleans	Imperial	°	°	
7/60	Don't Come Knockin'	Imperial			
9/60	Three Nights a Week	Imperial	°	°	
9/60	Put Your Arms Around Me Honey	Imperial			
10/60	My Girl Josephine	Imperial	°	°	
1/61	Natural Born Lover	Imperial			
1/61	Ain't That Just Like a Woman	Imperial		°	
1/61	What a Price	Imperial		°	
3/61	Shu Rah	Imperial			
3/61	Fall in Love on Monday	Imperial			
5/61	It Keeps Rainin'	Imperial		°	
7/61	Let the Four Winds Blow	Imperial	°	°	
10/61	Rockin' Bicycle	Imperial			
12/61	Jambalaya (on the Bayou)	Imperial			
12/61	I Hear You Knockin'	Imperial			
2/62	You Win Again	Imperial			
3/62	Ida Jane	Imperial			
5/62	My Real Name	Imperial			
7/62	Dance with Mr. Domino	Imperial			
10/62	Did You Ever See a Dream Walking	Imperial			
5/63	There Goes (My Heart Again)	Imperial			
9/63	Red Sails in the Sunset	ABC			
9/68	Lady Madonna	Reprise			

ALBUMS

Date	Album	Label
7/62	*Million Sellers By Fats*	Imperial
10/63	*Here Comes Fats Domino*	ABC Paramount
10/68	*Fats Is Back*	Reprise

LITTLE RICHARD

Little Richard, more than any other performer of the fifties, epitomizes the wild and uninhibited nature of rock 'n' roll. His intense singing and frantic movements have influenced every performer from Jerry Lee Lewis to the Rolling Stones. Some of his songs have become rock 'n' roll standards. Many of them were recorded by Elvis, the Beatles, and a host of other rock 'n' rollers. Richard was the most flamboyant performer of his era. Dressing in loud costumes, with flashy jewelry and shiny processed hair, he draped his leg across the piano and screamed his songs with the frenzied joy of a revival preacher.

Richard Penniman was born in Macon, Georgia, in 1932, the third of fourteen children. At age seven, Richard began singing in the streets for nickels and dimes. When he was fourteen, he was the lead singer of the local church choir. In 1951, Little Richard won a talent show in Atlanta, which led to a recording contract with RCA. The results were several unexciting and unsuccessful

Little Richard (Courtesy of Columbia Pictures)

blues records. In 1953, he moved to the Peacock label in Houston, where he recorded some crying blues songs. These records also did not sell. When Art Rupe of Specialty Records bought his contract in 1955, Little Richard was working as a dishwasher in the Macon bus station. It was there that he wrote his first hits—"Tutti Frutti," "Good Golly Miss Molly," and "Long Tall Sally."

"Tutti Frutti," released in late 1955, was the first of a series of songs in the exciting gospel-blues style of Little Richard. He was, perhaps, the first popular performer to take the music of the black church and turn it into rock 'n' roll. Richard believed in the religious power of his music. He called it "the healing music, the music that makes the blind see, and the lame walk."

In 1956 and 1957, Little Richard turned out one powerhouse rock 'n' roll record after another. "Rip It Up," "Slippin' and Slidin'," "Jenny Jenny," "Ready Teddy," and "Keep A-Knockin'" are some of his well-known songs. During this time Richard appeared in a good movie about rock 'n' roll called *The Girl Can't Help It* and sang the title song. Although his records were widely known, only "Long Tall Sally" was a big hit on the pop charts. Many disc jockeys considered his uninhibited singing and performing too extreme and banned his records.

Inevitably, many imitators attempted songs in the Little Richard style. Esquerita captured some of Little Richard's wild approach on several Capitol recordings—"Rockin' the Joint" and "Batty Over Hattie" are two examples. Larry Williams wrote similar songs and was recorded by the same producer, Art Rupe. Williams had several hits, most notably, "Short Fat Fanny" and "Bony Marony." His records resembled the high-spirited style of Little Richard, but Williams sang in a much more controlled manner.

Little Richard stopped recording and performing rock 'n' roll in 1958, but he did it in a way that was all his own. He abruptly announced that he was leaving the world of show business to become a minister. Many people who knew him believed that Richard took the launching of Sputnik as a sign from heaven. Richard enrolled in a Seventh-Day Adventist School.

Little Richard remained true to his religious vows for several years. When he went back to recording, he sang only gospel songs. But, in time, Richard began performing rock 'n' roll again. In the last few years, he has recorded several albums, appeared in the movie, *Let the Good Times Roll,* and performed in various oldies shows.

The same spirit and energy that helped to launch rock 'n' roll can be heard in Vegas nightclubs and on national television shows. Little Richard still puts his foot across the piano. He still shouts, "Oh mah soul wheeeoooo" and still sings, "Awa bob-a-loo bop-awap-bam-boom." The man who helped change the world in the fifties is still rockin' and rollin'.

LITTLE RICHARD COLLECTORS' GUIDE

—Smash hit in that category

Date	Song	Label	Pop	R&B	C&W
12/55	Tutti-Frutti	Specialty	*	*	
3/56	Long Tall Sally	Specialty	*	*	
4/56	Slippin' and Slidin'	Specialty		*	
6/56	Rip It Up	Specialty		*	
6/56	Ready Teddy	Specialty		*	
10/56	She Got It/Heeby Jeebies	Specialty		*	
1/57	The Girl Can't Help It	Specialty		*	
3/57	Lucille/Send Me Some Lovin'	Specialty		*	
6/57	Jenny, Jenny/Miss Ann	Specialty	*	*	
9/57	Keep A-Knockin'	Specialty	*	*	
2/58	Good Golly Miss Molly	Specialty	*	*	
5/58	Ooh! My Soul/True Fine Mamma	Specialty		*	
9/58	Baby Face	Specialty		*	
5/59	Kansas City	Specialty			
11/65	I Don't Know What You've Got But It's Got Me	Vee Jay		*	

ALBUMS

Date	Album	Label
7/57	*Here's Little Richard*	Specialty
8/67	*Little Richard's Greatest Hits*	Okeh
11/71	*King of Rock and Roll*	Reprise

ROCKABILLY

A group of singers from Memphis created a combination of country music and rhythm and blues that came to be known as country-rock. In contrast to the music of Bill Haley, the rockabilly singers integrated these musical styles in a much more consistent and original way. The style developed under the creative supervision of Sam Phillips, a Memphis record store owner. Phillips began his career in the record business by producing local blues singers like B. B. King and Howlin' Wolf and leasing the masters to companies like Chess and Modern. When some of these records turned a profit, Phillips set up his own label which he called Sun. Shortly thereafter, two of the new company's artists, Junior Parker and Rufus Thomas, had R&B hits.

The Memphis blues singers used small combos that featured piano, guitar, and saxophone. Phillips carefully developed the individual styles of his artists. Many of these records became popular among teenagers in the South. These Memphis blues records seemed to capture the spirit of the young southern audience better than traditional country and western music.

Elvis Presley was the first white singer to record for Sun in what Sam Phillips called the "documentary" or "personal" Sun style. Presley recorded established blues songs like "Big Boy" Crudup's "That's All Right (Mama)" and Junior Parker's "Mystery Train." These blues sides were always backed by traditional country material like "Blue Moon of Kentucky" and "You're a Heartbreaker."

Not all of the Memphis rockabilly singers were as interested in the blues as Elvis. Johnny Cash, and even Carl Perkins, sang in a more traditional country style. But the dance beat on their records came from rhythm and blues. For the most part, country-rock bands had no saxophones or chorus singing from the musicians. Like the New Orleans singers, the country rockers were personal and confiding in their singing styles. But in contrast to the warm tenor sax solos that mirrored the singer's mood in New Orleans rock 'n' roll, country-rock records usually featured exciting lead guitar players who responded to sudden shifts in the singer's emotions. This give and take between musician and singer is apparent

The Prisonaires—a gospel group from a Memphis prison—recorded on location by Sam Phillips of Sun Records ("Bleecker" Bob Plotnik Collection)

on the early Sun cuts between Elvis and guitar player Scotty Moore.

The first million seller in the Sun rockabilly style was Carl Perkins's "Blue Suede Shoes," in January 1956. In April of that year, Johnny Cash had Sun's second pop hit, "I Walk the Line." This record was closer to conventional country music than to rock 'n' roll. Another Memphis rocker, Jerry Lee Lewis, had several big hits in 1956–57. Lewis, with his boogie-style piano playing, and flashy performing, was reminiscent of Little Richard.

By 1957, rockabilly had become a major force in America's popular music. It had achieved commercial success in a variety of styles. Other labels throughout the country began to record performers in these country-rock styles. Some of the singers who achieved some success in the country-rock vein were Gene Vincent and the Blue Caps, Eddie Cochran, Charlie Rich, Dale Hawkins, Ronnie Hawkins, and Roy Orbison.

Roy Orbison and the Teen Kings (Billy Vera Collection)

Aside from the Memphis crowd, two acts from other parts of the country established successful careers in the country-rock style. These were Buddy Holly, who was influenced by an Elvis performance he attended in Lubbock, Texas, and the Everly Brothers, who had been performing country music all their lives.

ROCKABILLY COLLECTORS' GUIDE

Year	Song	Artist	Label
1958	Ballad of a Teenage Queen	Johnny Cash	Sun
1959	Forty Days	Ronnie Hawkins	Roulette
1959	Mary Lou	Ronnie Hawkins	Roulette
1959	La-Do-Dada	Dale Hawkins	Checker
1957	Lotta Lovin'	Gene Vincent	Capitol
1956	I Walk the Line	Johnny Cash	Sun
1958	Guess Things Happen That Way	Johnny Cash	Sun
1958	The Ways of a Woman in Love	Johnny Cash	Sun
1956	Race with the Devil	Gene Vincent	Capitol

CARL PERKINS

Carl Perkins was the first of the Memphis rockabilly singers to have a million-selling rock 'n' roll record. "Blue Suede Shoes," released in January 1956, was an immediate hit. In a short time it was riding on top of the R&B, country, and pop charts. The song, written by Perkins, has become one of the classic rock 'n' roll songs of all times. "Blue Suede Shoes" captured the mood of teenagers perhaps more than any other song of that time. The song said, you can take my money, take my car, do anything you want to my house, but don't step on my blue suede shoes. Somehow, these words expressed the newly discovered sense of identity teenagers were feeling. An outrageous pair of shoes, one that the older generation would frown upon, meant a great deal to young people in those days. (Perkins claims that he wrote the song about poor country boys being so proud of their new city-bought shoes.)

Born in Jackson, Tennessee, in 1932, Carl was the middle son of a poor sharecropping family. His first guitar was made by his fa-

Carl Perkins (Billy
Vera Collection)

ther out of a cigar box, a broomstick, and some wire. Carl got his
first real guitar at age five and was taught to play by a black migrant farmer called Uncle John. Perkins recalls joining the black
cotton pickers when they sang. That music, he remembers, was
rhythm and blues, later to be called rock 'n' roll.

When he was sixteen, Carl and his two brothers, Jay on rhythm
guitar and Clayton on bass, began working in local honky tonks.
By 1955 the Perkins brothers had made some tapes and were
sending them to various record companies. They received no response. One day, Carl heard a new singer named Elvis Presley
singing a "Big Boy" Crudup song called, "That's All Right
Mamma" on Sun Records. Perkins felt that he was in the same
musical mold as Elvis and tried to get an audition with Sun president Sam Phillips. At first, Phillips turned Carl down because his
sound was too close to Elvis's. But after Presley's record contract
was sold to RCA, Phillips sought a replacement with similar talents. He found a strong singer and guitar picker who could write
his own songs in Carl Perkins.

Perkins had equal skill as a writer and performer in rock 'n' roll as well as country music. Carl seemed to have everything going for him. He was young, talented and good-looking, and had a hit record that made him a hero of the new teen culture. "Blue Suede Shoes" outsold all of Elvis's Sun records by far; and Perkins claims to have upstaged Presley when the two performed at the same concert. But in 1956, Elvis became the greatest phenomenon in the history of the music business, and Carl Perkins faded from public attention.

Unfortunately for Carl, Presley recorded "Blue Suede Shoes" and made it the opening song on his new album. Elvis's version eclipsed Carl's in radio play and record sales. Although he made some money as the writer of the song, he was soon forgotten by a fickle public. Many people still regard "Blue Suede Shoes" as an Elvis Presley song.

Another piece of bad luck was to inflict itself on Carl Perkins. On March 22, 1956, while driving to New York to appear on the Ed Sullivan and Perry Como shows, Carl and his band were victims of a car crash. The accident, which eventually claimed the life of his rhythm-playing brother Jay, removed Perkins from the limelight for several months. By the time Carl got out of the hospital, Elvis's version of "Blue Suede Shoes" was just one of his many hits. Carl's managers waited eight months to release his second single, but he never had another big hit.

Perkins recorded seven records for Sun. All were fast rock 'n' roll songs backed by country and western ballads. On the fast songs, Carl used a strong boogie-woogie-based beat and a rough vocal sound. On the country songs, his smooth singing was typical of many performers.

Carl Perkins's lasting influence is as a songwriter and guitarist. The Beatles recorded three of his songs on their early albums: "Honey Don't," "Matchbox," and "Everybody's Tryin' to Be My Baby." The seventies rock group NRBQ has recorded some of Carl's tunes and featured his guitar playing on several of their albums. Guitarists like George Harrison and Jerry Garcia gratefully acknowledge Perkins's influence on their playing.

Columbia Records has recently released a new Carl Perkins album, *Old Blue Suede Shoes Is Back.* In recent years, Carl has traveled with the Johnny Cash road show. He has been opening for Cash and backing him as a featured guitarist. Although Perkins works steadily and makes a good living, it is difficult for a person to reach the top and then have to settle for something less. Carl Perkins is not a bitter man, but he has said, "I've been at the bottom of the bill and on the top; and believe me, the top beats the bottom every time."

CARL PERKINS COLLECTORS' GUIDE
°—Smash hit in that category

Date	Song	Label	Pop	R&B	C&W
2/56	Blue Suede Shoes	Sun	°	°	°
7/56	Boppin' the Blues	Sun	°		°
9/56	Dixie Fried/I'm Sorry, I'm Not Sorry	Sun			°
3/57	Your True Love	Sun			°
5/58	Pink Pedal Pushers	Columbia			°
6/59	Pointed Toe Shoes	Columbia			
1/69	Restless	Columbia			°

ALBUMS

Date	Album	Label
1978	*Old Blue Suede Shoes is Back*	Columbia

ELVIS PRESLEY

The Elvis Presley explosion in 1956 was probably one of the most important cultural events in American history. He embodied the spirit of rock 'n' roll more than any other performer. His importance goes far beyond his groundbreaking performances on the Sun label. Certainly, there were other white singers who stepped into the forbidden territory of black music. But no other white singer of that time was able to bring as much as Elvis did to blues singing.

Presley was much more than a white singer trying to copy black sound. He had a unique and inventive style of blues interpretation. Singing in an excited and impatient manner, Elvis altered the lyrics and emotions of the original blues records until they became his own personal statements. He was at his best on fast songs like

Elvis on stage with guitarist Scotty Moore (Billy Vera Collection)

Arthur "Big Boy" Crudup's "That's All Right (Mama)" and Junior Parker's "Mystery Train." Instead of using the blues to express sadness or feeling down, Elvis seemed to find an expression for his own confidence and freedom.

Sam Phillips, who owned Sun Records, had been searching for a talent like Elvis for years. He knew that there was an ever-growing market for a white singer with a feel for black music. As legend has it, Elvis was overheard while making a record in one of those "record your voice" booths in Phillips's Memphis record store. He was overheard by Phillips's secretary, who urged Sam to listen to the unknown singer. Phillips liked what he heard, but spent months working with Elvis until he let him cut a record. His first release on Sun, "That's All Right Mamma," became a local hit. In a 1957 interview that appeared in the English magazine *Hit Parader*, Elvis recalls his earliest days with Sun:

> "You want to make some blues?" He [Phillips] suggested over the phone, knowing I'd always been a sucker for that kind of jive. He mentioned Big Boy Crudup's name and maybe others too. I don't remember.
>
> All I know is, I hung up and ran fifteen blocks to Mr. Phillips' office before he'd gotten off the line—or so he tells me. We talked about the Crudup records I knew—"Cool Disposition," "Rock Me Mama," "Hey Mama," "Everything's All Right," and others, but settled for "That's All Right," one of my top favorites.

The unique style of blues singing which Elvis achieved has to be credited, in part, to Phillips's skill in developing the personal styles of his artists. Presley cut five records for Sun. Each one was a blues song backed with a country and western song. Most of the material was already familiar to the local audience. Elvis's singing on the country sides was steeped in tradition and was similar to dozens of other country and western vocalists. On the other hand, the blues sides confused some of the southern audience. Many listeners called the music "hillbilly bop"; and others questioned the morality of a white man singing the blues. Even in those early days, some radio stations banned Elvis's records.

Born in 1935 in Tupelo, Mississippi, Elvis's first exposure to music came from the Pentecostal First Assembly of God Church. His family often attended revival sermons, which borrowed the gospel styles of the black Sanctified Church. Elvis recalled singing this music when he was two years old. Shortly thereafter, the Presleys moved to Memphis in the hopes of improving their finances. Elvis got his first guitar when he was eleven and began to imitate everything he heard on the radio. He learned country ballads, sentimental pop tunes, and religious spirituals. When no one was around, Elvis listened to the singing of Mississippi blues men like Big Bill Broonzy and Arthur Crudup, as well as the Memphis blues styles of Johnny Ace and Rufus Thomas. This music was considered sinful by many blacks as well as whites. But to Elvis, the blues were not only exciting, they became his way out of a poor, unskilled laborer's life. Eventually, they led him to unimagined fortune and fame.

By the time Elvis released his last Sun single, "Mystery Train," in 1955, his popularity had grown. He was now headlining his own show. Under the astute management of Colonel Tom Parker, Elvis performed for audiences from Florida to Texas. He even appeared at San Francisco's well-known Cow Palace Theater. During a performance at a convention of country and western disc jockeys, Elvis greatly impressed Steve Shoales of RCA. The New York–based company decided to buy Elvis's Sun contract for $35,000 (a huge sum at that time).

At RCA, Elvis came under the supervision of producer Chet Atkins. Elvis's Sun records had been sparsely produced by Phillips. They used only the exciting lead guitar of Scotty Moore and the pulsating bass of Bill Black, in addition to Elvis's voice and rhythm guitar. In an attempt to broaden Elvis's appeal, Atkins used a male vocal group (the Jordanaires), drums, and additional guitars. In response to these new arrangements, Elvis used a lower and more self-consciously dramatic vocal style. Still, many consider some of Elvis's early RCA records among his best. His first release on his new label was "Heartbreak Hotel" in February 1956.

That year belonged to Elvis. He kept turning out another multimillion selling record almost every few weeks. "Heartbreak Hotel" was followed by "Blue Suede Shoes" in March, "My Baby Left Me" in May, "I Want You, I Need You, I Love You" in May, and the two-sided smash, "Hound Dog"/"Don't Be Cruel" in July. As the year came to a close, Elvis appeared in his first movie, *Love Me Tender*, and had his first ballad hit with the title song.

Presley's popularity among the young was without precedent. He appeared on the network television shows of Steve Allen, Jackie Gleason, and Ed Sullivan. While Sullivan insisted that Presley wear a suit and be filmed only above the waist, Gleason and Allen placed no restrictions on his performance.

Elvis was here to stay. During the 104 weeks from 1956 to 1958, there was always at least one Elvis record on the charts. He was a living celebration of an American success story. He had burst out of his humble beginnings in shining gold Cadillacs. Several times he even drove a Cadillac onto the stage. His jewelry and glittering clothes went beyond the fantasies of any Hollywood movie. He was the undisputed king of rock 'n' roll.

In May 1958, Elvis was drafted into the army. His clean-cut soldier image made him much more acceptable to adults. He also appeared in a number of movies in which he sang more like a crooner than a rocker. When he got out of the army, he continued to make movies and release records like, "It's Now or Never" (an English version of the Italian sentimental ballad "O Sole Mio").

By the mid-sixties, Elvis had become a joke to the now grown-up and more sophisticated rock fan. He had seemingly become "the king of corn." Meanwhile, younger and more self-aware performers like the Beatles, the Rolling Stones, and Bob Dylan were dominating the scene. But Elvis was not finished.

In 1968, during an internationally televised Christmas special, Elvis staged a daring comeback. Appearing on the stage dressed in a black leather jacket and surrounded by his original band, Elvis

A familiar promo shot of Elvis in the seventies (Courtesy of *Record World* magazine)

showed that he could still deliver with the best. He was still the King. After the television special, Elvis topped the charts again with "Suspicious Minds." He also began to perform live. His performances were a mixture of religious gospel music, country ballads, patriotic songs, and rock 'n' roll. He could move nimbly from "Battle Hymn of the Republic" to "Hound Dog" without batting an eyelash.

The importance of Elvis as a symbol of life in America is thoroughly explored by Greil Marcus in his remarkable book,

Mystery Train. Marcus concludes that "Elvis has survived contradictions of his career." But shortly after the publication of *Mystery Train* in 1976, Elvis underwent a personal decline which hindered his performance and eventually took his life.

In Elvis's final performance, which was taped and televised after his death in July 1977, we see an Elvis who has gained one hundred pounds and lost most of his ability to sing. There is still a great deal of mystery surrounding the causes of his death.

Although he is gone, Elvis has lost none of his appeal. There are Presley imitators galore who are making a living looking and sounding like Elvis. The demand for Presley's records is greater than ever. At a recent Elvis convention in New York, people paid $50 for a picture of the King. His movies are constantly being shown on television. Elvis Presley's importance goes far beyond even his best recordings. But for now the true lover of rock 'n' roll must settle for the joys that this great music still provides.

ELVIS PRESLEY COLLECTORS' GUIDE
•—Smash hit in that category

Date	Song	Label	Pop	R&B	C&W
/54	That's All Right Mama/Blue Moon of Kentucky	Sun			
/54	Good Rockin' Tonight/I Don't Care If the Sun Don't Shine	Sun			
/55	Milkcow Blues Boogie/You're a Heartbreaker	Sun			
/55	Baby Let's Play House/I'm Left, You're Right, She's Gone	Sun			•
/55	Mystery Train/I Forgot to Remember to Forget	Sun			•
2/56	Heartbreak Hotel/I Was the One	RCA	•	•	•
3/56	Blue Suede Shoes	RCA	•		
5/56	I Want You, I Need You, I Love You/My Baby Left Me	RCA	•	•	•
7/56	Don't Be Cruel	RCA	•	•	•
7/56	Hound Dog	RCA	•	•	•
10/56	Love Me Tender/Anyway You Want Me (That's How I Will Be)	RCA	•	•	•

Date	Song	Label	Pop	R&B	C&W
11/56	Love Me/When My Blue Moon Turns to Gold Again	RCA	*		
12/56	Poor Boy	RCA			
12/56	Old Shep	RCA			
1/57	Too Much/Playing for Keeps	RCA	*	*	*
3/57	All Shook Up/That's When Your Heartaches Begin	RCA	*	*	*
3/57	(There'll Be) Peace in the Valley	RCA			
6/57	Let Me Be Your Teddy Bear/Loving You	RCA	*	*	*
10/57	Jailhouse Rock	RCA	*	*	*
10/57	Treat Me Nice	RCA	*	*	*
1/58	Don't/I Beg of You	RCA	*	*	*
4/58	Wear My Ring Around Your Neck/Doncha' Think Its Time	RCA	*	*	*
6/58	Hard Headed Woman/Don't Ask Me Why	RCA	*	*	*
11/58	One Night/I Got Stung	RCA	*	*	
11/58	(Now and Then There's) A Fool Such as I?/I Need Your Love Tonight	RCA	*	*	
7/59	A Big Hunk o' Love/My Wish Came True	RCA	*	*	
4/60	Stuck on You/Fame and Fortune	RCA	*	*	
7/60	It's Now or Never/A Mess of Blues	RCA	*	*	
11/60	Are You Lonesome Tonight/I Gotta Know	RCA	*	*	
2/61	Surrender	RCA	*		
4/61	Flaming Star	RCA	*		
5/61	I Feel So Bad/Wild in the Streets	RCA	*	*	
8/61	(Marie's the Name) His Latest Flame/Little Sister	RCA	*		
12/61	Can't Help Falling in Love/Rock-a-Hula Baby	RCA	*		
3/62	Good Luck Charm/Anything That's Part of You	RCA	*		
5/62	Follow That Dream	RCA	*		
9/62	She's Not You	RCA	*	*	
9/62	King of the Whole Wide World	RCA			
10/62	Return to Sender	RCA	*	*	
2/63	One Broken Heart for Sale	RCA	*		

Date	Song	Label	Pop	R&B	C&W
6/63	(You're the) Devil in Disguise	RCA	°	°	
10/63	Bossa Nova Baby/Witchcraft	RCA	°	°	
2/64	Kissin' Cousins/It Hurts Me	RCA	°		
7/64	Such a Night	RCA	°		
10/64	Ask Me/Ain't That Loving You	RCA	°		
4/65	Crying in the Chapel	RCA	°		
6/65	(Such an) Easy Question	RCA	°		
9/65	I'm Yours	RCA	°		
11/65	Puppet on a String	RCA	°		
7/66	Love Letters	RCA	°		
11/68	If I Can Dream	RCA	°		
5/69	In the Ghetto	RCA	°		
9/69	Suspicious Minds	RCA	°		
11/69	Don't Cry Daddy	RCA	°		°
2/70	Kentucky Rain	RCA	°		
5/70	The Wonder of You	RCA	°		
10/70	You Don't Have to Say You Love Me	RCA	°		
12/70	I Really Don't Want to Know	RCA	°		°
9/72	Burning Love	RCA	°		
12/72	Separate Ways	RCA	°		
5/73	Steamroller Blues/Fool	RCA	°		
/75	Trouble	RCA			°

ALBUMS

Date	Album	Label
4/12/58	*Elvis's Golden Records*	RCA Victor
2/19/60	*Elvis's Golden Records Volume 2*	RCA Victor
9/14/63	*Elvis's Golden Records Volume 3*	RCA Victor
3/2/68	*Elvis's Golden Records Volume 4*	RCA Victor
8/22/70	*Elvis's 50 Worldwide Gold Award Hits, Volume 1*	RCA Victor
8/22/71	*Elvis's 50 Worldwide Gold Award Hits, Volume 2*	RCA Victor

JERRY LEE LEWIS

Jerry Lee Lewis was born in Ferraday, Louisiana, in 1935. Encouraged by his parents, he began playing the piano at age nine. As a teenager, he worked his first professional engagement at the Blue Cat Club in Natchez, Mississippi. After that, he worked steadily at the Wagon Wheel Club, singing and playing piano. Jerry Lee's first musical idol was Al Jolson. When he heard a record of Jolson singing "Down Among the Sheltering Pines," he ran home and reproduced it on the piano. Lewis still considers Jolson the number one performer of all time.

As a youth, Jerry Lee and his cousin would sneak into the local black nightclub and listen intently to Ray Charles, B. B. King, Bobby "Blue" Bland, and other rhythm and blues greats. At the same time he listened to the country records of Jimmie Rodgers and Hank Williams that his father brought home. These musical influences were combined with a strong background in church music. Jerry Lee had even considered becoming a preacher at one time.

In 1956, Lewis was one of the many young singers from the rural South who journeyed to Memphis to audition for Sun Records. Sam Phillips had recently sold Elvis's Sun contract to RCA, and performers like Jerry Lee realized that there was a market for their kind of music. Lewis's first Sun release was a remake of "Crazy Arms," which had recently been a country hit for Ray Price. The record had some local success, but it was Jerry Lee's second record that really launched his career.

"Whole Lotta Shakin' Goin' On" was recorded almost by accident. Jerry Lee and his group were working on another song in the studio when he suggested that Sun executive Jack Clement listen to an original tune that Lewis had been playing around with. Without any rehearsal, Jerry Lee recorded the song in one take. The result was one of the greatest rock 'n' roll records of all time.

Released in June of 1957, "Whole Lotta Shakin' Goin' On" reached the top of the pop, country and western, and rhythm and blues charts. Over six million copies have been sold to date. Jerry Lee appeared on the Steve Allen television show later in the year, and his dynamic performance turned him into a major concert at-

Jerry Lee Lewis (Neal Hollander Collection)

traction. Lewis's wild stage act and frenzied piano style owed much to Little Richard. His vocal style, unlike Little Richard's, was quite controlled. Lewis was able to build his vocals to a fever pitch and suddenly drop down to a whisper. This technique allowed Lewis to control the emotions of his live audiences.

In the latter part of 1957, a New York songwriter named Otis Blackwell sent a demo of "Great Balls of Fire" to Sun. Lewis rehearsed the tune once and then recorded it within five minutes. The result was another smash hit, with sales going well over the five million mark. By 1958, Jerry Lee had his third hit, "Breathless." Lewis was now so popular that he sold out five shows a day at the New York Paramount Theater. In doing so, he broke every attendance record, including Frank Sinatra's.

Jerry Lee Lewis's career was exploding. He appeared in a movie, *High School Confidential*, and sang the title song. Jerry Lee was outgoing and somewhat rash. He always insisted that he close every show, believing that nobody was good enough to follow him. Once at an Alan Freed rock 'n' roll show that also starred Chuck Berry, Lewis insisted on closing the show. Both artists were extremely popular at the time, but Freed chose Berry as the last act. After a long argument, Jerry Lee yielded. It is said that Lewis played a most intense set. During his last number, he poured lighter fluid over the piano and put a match to it. As he jumped off the stage, he yelled that he'd like to see anyone follow that.

The roof caved in on Jerry Lee's career toward the end of 1958. While he was on tour in London the British press began running stories about his recent marriage to his thirteen-year-old cousin, Myra. Although such marriages were not uncommon in the South, Lewis was pictured as a dangerous person by those who resented rock 'n' roll. When he returned to the United States, he found his records banned by many radio stations and his concert dates canceled.

During the next ten years Jerry Lee worked in clubs all over the country. In 1963, he left Sun and signed with Smash Records. Lewis never had another rock 'n' roll hit single, but he did record a great live album, *The Greatest Live Show on Earth*. In 1968, Jerry Lee consented to record only country and western material. He soon had a top ten C&W hit with, "Another Place Another Time." His records get consistent air play on country stations.

Today, Jerry Lee Lewis is a very successful country and western artist and does a few fifties revival shows as well. He appeared in the 1978 movie, *American Hot Wax* along with Chuck Berry. He still likes to close his shows with "Whole Lotta Shakin' Goin' On." Of all the rockabilly singers to come out of Memphis, Jerry Lee Lewis is second only to Elvis.

JERRY LEE LEWIS COLLECTORS' GUIDE
°—Smash hit in that category

Date	Song	Label	Pop	R&B	C&W
6/57	Whole Lotta Shakin' Goin' on	Sun	°	°	°
11/57	Great Balls of Fire	Sun	°	°	°
2/58	You Win Again	Sun			
2/58	Breathless	Sun	°	°	°
2/58	High School Confidential	Sun	°	°	°
9/58	Breakup	Sun			
9/58	I'll Make It All Up to You	Sun			°
1/59	I'll Sail My Ship Alone	Sun			
4/61	What'd I Say	Sun	°		
8/61	Cold Cold Heart	Sun			
9/62	Sweet Little Sixteen	Sun			

ALBUMS

Date	Album	Label
3/28/64	*The Golden Hits of Jerry Lee Lewis*	Smash
12/5/64	*The Greatest Live Show on Earth*	Smash
9/27/69	*Original Golden Hits Volume 1*	Sun
9/27/69	*Original Golden Hits Volume 2*	Sun

BUDDY HOLLY

Of all the early rock 'n' roll performers, one of the most influential was Buddy Holly. The Beatles were strongly influenced by him. Paul McCartney purchased the entire Holly song catalog sev-

Buddy Holly (Courtesy of *Record World* magazine)

eral years ago. The Rolling Stones' first American single was a Holly song, "Not Fade Away," and Bob Dylan admits his debt to Holly's vocal phrasing. Although Holly never had a number one hit, he had seven songs on the American charts in 1957 and 1958. In England he was even more popular. His effect on the English groups of the mid-sixties is just now being fully recognized.

Since the release of the film, *The Buddy Holly Story* in 1978, there has been a growing interest in his life. There is some disagreement between the film's producers and Holly's friends about certain events, but there are some known facts about his life.

Charles Hardin Holly was born in Lubbock, Texas, in 1936. At age five he sang in his first talent show. Three years later, he began to study violin and piano, but soon switched to guitar. At thirteen, Buddy and his friend Bob Montgomery began working local clubs as a duo. Buddy and Bob became quite popular playing a style of music which they called western bop. The duo recorded a conventional country album, but got little response. But when Buddy and his band opened for Bill Haley at a local rock 'n' roll show, Buddy was signed by Decca Records.

The first few records that Holly cut for Decca were not considered commercial, so he returned to Lubbock to work on some new material. Several months later, Buddy hooked up with producer Norman Petty, who owned a recording studio in Clovis, New Mexico. Petty had already achieved commercial success with Buddy Knox ("Party Doll") and Jimmy Bowen ("I'm Stickin' with You"). But the sides Petty cut with Holly far surpassed anything that he had ever done.

Some of Holly's records were released under his own name on the Coral label, while a second series was released on the Brunswick label under the group name, the Crickets. The group consisted of Holly on guitar and lead vocal, Jerry Allison on drums, Joe B. Mauldin on bass, and Niki Sullivan on rhythm guitar. The Crickets' first release, "That'll Be the Day," established the group's sound and Holly's unique vocal style. Buddy's first solo release was "Peggy Sue," which became his biggest hit. Holly's singing created a lot of excitement. He used vocal techniques like stretching out syllables and hiccups to great effect. The Crickets' records sometimes used a backup vocal group called the Roses. The music that resulted was an exciting mixture of electric guitars, voices, and rhythm. On top of these textures rode Holly's unique voice.

There are different stories concerning which Crickets did what. Some sources deny that Holly was his own record producer. There is also some disagreement as to Petty's role. Although the recent film does not even mention Petty, most sources agree that he cowrote some of the tunes, played keyboard, and produced most of the Crickets' hits.

In the summer of 1958, Buddy met Maria Elena Santiago, who worked in the office of his publishers, Peer-Southern. Several weeks later, the two were married. After the wedding, the Hollys moved to New York City. Around the same time, Buddy split with the Crickets and producer Petty. With new producer Dick Jacobs, Holly began to make records in a much softer style. He experimented with strings in the Paul Anka song, "It Doesn't Matter

Anymore," and his own composition, "Raining in My Heart." These were to be his final recordings.

In January 1959, Buddy began a tour with Dion and the Belmonts, Richie Valens, and the Big Bopper. Backing up Holly on the tour were Waylon Jennings on bass, Tommy Alsup on lead guitar, and Charles Bunch on drums. The performers had been traveling by bus, but Holly decided to charter a plane to the next town in order to save time. His backup band took the bus, but Valens and the Big Bopper chose to go with Holly. The plane crashed, and all those aboard perished. That day, February 3, 1959, is still remembered as "the day the music died."

As is so often the case, Holly's records seemed to become much more important after his death. Many imitators appeared almost immediately. They were led by Bobby Vee, who recorded the album, *I Remember Buddy*. In recent years, artists like Linda Ronstadt have done well re-recording Holly's songs. Because of the film, there will probably be an even greater interest in Holly's work. His contributions to the modern rock scene were many. Malcolm Jones, writing in a British rock magazine, described Holly's influence:

> Holly scored with a dazzling series of firsts in an era where everyone followed the flock. He was the first white rock star to rely almost exclusively on his own material. The Crickets were probably the first white group to feature the lead/rhythm/bass/drum lineup. He was the first rock singer to double-track his voice and guitar. He was the first to use strings on a rock 'n' roll record. In addition, he popularized the Fender Stratocaster [guitar] and was probably the only rock star to wear glasses onstage!

BUDDY HOLLY COLLECTORS' GUIDE
—Smash hit in that category

Date	Song	Label	Pop	R&B	C&W
11/57	Peggy Sue	Coral	*	*	
5/58	Rave On	Coral			
8/58	Early in the Morning	Coral			
1/59	Heartbeat	Coral			
3/59	It Doesn't Matter Anymore	Coral	*		
4/59	Raining in My Heart	Coral			

BUDDY HOLLY AND THE CRICKETS
COLLECTORS' GUIDE

Date	Song	Label	Pop	R&B	C&W
8/57	That'll Be the Day	Brunswick	°	°	
1/58	Oh Boy	Brunswick	°	°	
2/58	Maybe Baby	Brunswick	°	°	
7/58	Think It Over	Brunswick			
8/58	Fool's Paradise	Brunswick			

ALBUMS

Date	Album	Label
4/59	*The Buddy Holly Story*	Coral
3/63	*Reminiscing*	Coral

THE EVERLY BROTHERS

The Everly Brothers were the most commercially successful country-rock singers outside of the Sun artists. Their sound was derived from the close harmony style of country and western music. Compared with Elvis and even Buddy Holly, the Everlys sounded like choir boys. Nevertheless, their vocal sound clearly influenced the Beach Boys, the Mamas and the Papas, Crosby, Stills, Nash, and Young, and the Beatles. In fact, before they became the Beatles, McCartney, Lennon, and friends called themselves the Everlys. Phil and Don's records have been successfully re-recorded by Linda Ronstadt, "When Will I Be Loved?"; Donny Osmond, "Bye Bye Love"; Bob Dylan, "Take a Message to Mary"; and James Taylor–Carly Simon, "Devoted to You."

Phil and Don Everly were eighteen and twenty years old, respectively, when they recorded their first hit, "Bye Bye Love." Their parents, Margaret and Ike, were well-known country artists with their own radio show in Shenandoah, Iowa. When Phil was six and Don eight, they made their first radio appearance. After high school, the boys moved to Nashville and signed with Cadence Records. Guitarist–record producer Chet Atkins, who supervised Elvis's early sessions at RCA, became the brothers' producer. He

Don (*left*) and Phil Everly upon graduation from Marine Corps Training School (Courtesy of *Record World* magazine)

provided the Everlys' records with a distinctive instrumental sound that featured rich and percussive acoustic guitar work.

Early in their career, the Everlys met songwriters Boudeleaux and Felice Bryant and formed a close relationship with them. The Bryants wrote most of the Everlys' big hits. Boudeleaux had been a member of the string section of the Atlanta Symphony Orchestra, an unusual background for a rock 'n' roll songwriter. Nevertheless, he penned the brothers' first record, "Bye Bye Love." The tune was a snappy shuffle that rose to the top of the charts in 1957. Their second hit, "Wake Up Little Susie," released a few months later, shot up to number one in only four weeks.

"Wake Up Little Susie" was a song that captured a true predicament of teenage life. The song told of Susie and her boyfriend, who innocently fell asleep while watching a boring movie. The couple then had to face the girl's angry and suspicious parents. "Wake Up Little Susie" was banned in Boston and other areas where the lyrics were considered too suggestive. The ban was, apparently, widespread; "Bye Bye Love" made the top ten that year while "Susie" did not.

The Everlys continued to have big hits through 1962. Some of their records discussed various aspects of teenage life, while others were more mature in their outlook. One of their best records, "Till I Kissed You," was in the second category. Penned by Don in 1959 while he was in Australia, the song was recorded in Nashville with Buddy Holly's old band, the Crickets. On this session, Crickets drummer Joe Mauldin aggressively used a full set of drums, including tom-toms. Prior to this, it had been customary to use only a snare and bass drum. The song was released that summer and became a smash hit. In 1960 the Everlys recorded the ballad "Let It Be Me" in a New York studio. It was the first time they had recorded outside Nashville and the first time they used a string section on one of their records.

The brothers left Cadence in 1960 and signed with Warner Brothers. Their first release on the new label, "Cathy's Clown," was their all-time biggest selling record. Don and Phil were able to maintain their popularity throughout the mid- and late sixties. They recorded an interesting album, *Roots,* in 1968. This record combined tapes of the two young boys singing on their parents' radio show with modern-sounding country-rock music.

With the rise of folk-rock in the late sixties, the Everlys often appeared at clubs and concerts around the country. Their performances were energetic and high-spirited. In late 1973, the brothers split up to pursue individual recording careers.

THE EVERLY BROTHERS
COLLECTORS' GUIDE
—Smash hit in that category

Date	Song	Label	Pop	R&B	C&W
5/57	Bye Bye Love	Cadence	*	*	*
9/57	Wake Up Little Susie	Cadence	*	*	*
2/58	This Little Girl of Mine	Cadence			*
4/58	All I Have to Do Is Dream	Cadence		*	*
4/58	Claudette	Cadence			
8/58	Bird Dog	Cadence	*		*
8/58	Devoted to You	Cadence	*		*
11/58	Problems	Cadence	*		*

Date	Song	Label	Pop	R&B	C&W
11/58	Love of My Life	Cadence	°		
4/59	Take a Message to Mary	Cadence	°		
4/59	Poor Jenny	Cadence	°		
8/59	Till I Kissed You	Cadence	°		
1/60	Let It Be Me	Cadence	°		
6/60	When Will I Be Loved	Cadence	°		
7/60	Be-Bop-a-Lula	Cadence			
11/60	Like Strangers	Cadence			
7/61	All I Have to Do Is Dream	Cadence	°	°	°
10/62	I'm Here to Get My Baby Out of Jail	Cadence			
4/60	Cathy's Clown	Warner Brothers	°		
5/60	Always It's You	Warner Brothers			
9/60	So Sad	Warner Brothers	°	°	
9/60	Lucille	Warner Brothers			
2/61	Walk Right Back	Warner Brothers	°		
2/61	Ebony Eyes	Warner Brothers	°		
6/61	Temptation	Warner Brothers			
6/61	Stick with Me Baby	Warner Brothers			
10/61	Don't Blame Me	Warner Brothers	°		
10/61	Muskrat	Warner Brothers			
1/62	Crying in the Rain	Warner Brothers	°		
5/62	That's Old-Fashioned	Warner Brothers	°		

ALBUMS

Date	Album	Label
2/58	*The Everly Brothers*	Cadence
8/60	*The Fabulous Style of the Everly Brothers*	Cadence
5/60	*It's Everly Time*	Warner Brothers

Date	Album	Label
12/60	*A Date with the Everlys*	Warner Brothers
8/62	*The Golden Hits of the Everly Brothers*	Warner Brothers
9/65	*Beat and Soul*	Warner Brothers
7/70	*Original Greatest Hits*	Barnaby

CHICAGO STYLE ROCK 'N' ROLL

The Chicago style of rock 'n' roll was popularized by Chuck Berry and Bo Diddley. Both of these men were influenced by Chicago blues musicians like Muddy Waters and Howlin' Wolf. The loud and tough Chicago bar-blues did not appeal much to white audiences in the fifties. But Leonard Chess, who recorded many of the Chicago bluesmen, felt that Berry and Diddley were performers who had potential for reaching the white market. Chess Records released Diddley's "Bo Diddley" in April 1955 and Berry's "Maybellene" in June 1955. Both records became hits that year.

Chuck Berry, whom many consider the major figure of early rock 'n' roll, never made another record like "Maybellene." Supposedly co-written by Alan Freed and another disc jockey, "Maybellene" was similar to the records of Bill Haley and the Comets. Berry's later records, however, were closer in style to rockabilly than to Chicago blues. Arnold Shaw, in his book, *The Rockin' Fifties* aptly describes the similarities between the music of Elvis Presley and Chuck Berry: "Musically, Berry came from the opposite direction as Presley to meet almost at the crossroads of rockabilly. As Presley was a Memphis white singing guttural bluesy black, Berry was a St. Louis black singing country white." Shaw and many other historians believe that the "whiteness" of Berry's singing helped him to get pop air play before many of his black contemporaries.

There was no way that listeners could have mistaken the racial identity of Bo Diddley's music. This was clearly a black man sing-

Muddy Waters
(Courtesy of *Record World* magazine)

ing to a sensual and provocative beat. Although his records did not receive a great deal in pop air play, Diddley's records did rank high in sales and jukebox plays. His records were among the best dance music of the fifties. Oddly enough, many black listeners felt that the beat on Bo Diddley's records was too primitive, and avoided them.

Both Diddley and Chuck Berry recorded blues records with other Chicago-based blues musicians after they became established. Berry still includes slow blues numbers like "In the Wee Wee Hours" in his concerts, while both men have appeared on albums with musicians like harmonica player Little Walter.

Whereas the Chicago-blues artists were quite popular with the R&B audiences of the fifties, they rarely crossed over into pop. The music played by transplanted rural performers like Muddy Waters and Elmore James was originally labeled too crude for black audiences. Much to the surprise of record company owners like Leonard Chess, the music was very popular among black listeners. It was not, however, until the late sixties and seventies that these blues performers became well known among white audiences. This belated popularity was, in part, due to the tribute that rock-star guitar players like Eric Clapton, Jimi Hendrix, and Johnny Winter paid to these men. Although many of these great blues performers have passed on, their music is enjoying a period of great popularity.

Once the blues revival got under way in the late sixties, Chuck Berry began featuring Chicago blues numbers in his live perform-ances. When one hears these songs mixed in with Berry classics like, "Oh Carol" and "Johnny B. Goode," the connection between blues and rock 'n' roll becomes apparent.

CHUCK BERRY

Chuck Berry is probably the most influential rock 'n' roll guitar player. His style has affected rock guitar greats like Jimi Hendrix, Keith Richards, and Robbie Robertson. A number of his songs are rock 'n' roll classics. Many of them have been re-recorded by the Rolling Stones, the Beatles, the Beach Boys, and others. Though he was over thirty at the time, Chuck's songs captured the feelings of teenagers in the fifties. He was concerned with girls and cars ("Maybellene," "No Money Down"); growing up ("School Days,"

1957—Chuck Berry—1973 (Neal Hollander Collection)

"Almost Grown," "Sweet Little Sixteen"); and the importance of the music ("Roll Over Beethoven," "Rock and Roll Music").

Chuck was born in 1926. His high school glee club teacher in Wentzville, Missouri encouraged him to play the guitar, and in 1952 he formed his own group and began working bars in East St. Louis. Unable to support a wife and two daughters by playing the blues, Chuck took a day job as a hairdresser. The turning point in his career came during a 1955 vacation trip to Chicago.

Many blues men from the Deep South migrated to the South Side of Chicago. These included Muddy Waters, Elmore James, and Howlin' Wolf. One night, Muddy Waters let Berry sit in with his band. One of the songs Chuck played, "Ida Red," so impressed Waters he set up an audition with Chess Records. The result was the release of Chuck Berry's first hit single in July 1955.

Originally conceived as a country and western tune, "Ida Red" was changed to "Maybellene." The lyrics were about a guy in a V-8 Ford chasing his girl, who was rolling down the road in a coupe-de-ville Cadillac. The style and beat of "Maybellene" was similar to the songs of Bill Haley and the Comets. Alan Freed, who was at the recording session and claimed a writer's credit on "Maybellene," gave the song a good deal of exposure. "Maybellene" replaced "Rock Around the Clock" as the number one song on the rhythm and blues charts in 1955. On the pop charts, the song was one of the year's top fifty hits. Many rock historians feel that Berry's clear voice and pronunciation "passed for white" on radio stations that usually avoided rhythm and blues records.

Although Chuck maintained his clear singing style on later records, he discarded the northern band style of "Maybellene." Most of his hit songs featured a fast eight-note shuffle feel. They were characterized by piercing guitar licks in response to vocal phrases. Berry also loved to play the slow style of Chicago blues and even asked Leonard Chess's permission to record an album in this vein under an assumed name. Chess refused. He insisted that Berry stick to making records with the big beat.

The list of great Chuck Berry tunes is impressive. His unique musical style was given support by Johnny Johnson's rolling piano figures and Ebby Harding's pounding drum beat. Above all, the daring and insight of Berry's words stand out. No other writer-performer of that era was so aware of what the new music was about. Berry was a sympathetic observer who wrote about the lives of his listeners.

This poet of rock 'n' roll was, and still is, a great showman. He had suave good looks and a long lanky body. He paraded across the stage in a bouncing step he called the "duck walk." With perfect grace, he would squat down on one heel, stick his other leg out, and bounce across the stage. As he bounced, he would hold his guitar out and play it like a machine gun.

Berry is considered by many to be the most important figure in early rock 'n' roll. His musical style was as close to rockabilly as to Chicago blues. Just as Elvis and the other Memphis rockers were white southerners with a feel for rhythm and blues, Chuck was a black midwesterner with a strong country feel. In one of his most famous songs, "Johnny B. Goode," Berry tells of a young rock 'n' roll guitar virtuoso on his way up. This could easily be Buddy Holly's or Carl Perkins's biography as well as his own.

Today, Chuck Berry is still playing rock 'n' roll shows and still doing the "duck walk." He has many business interests in his home town of Wentzville, Missouri, including a large amusement park called Berry Park. He continues to record for Chess Records (now called All Platinum). He has been featured in the movies *Let the Good Times Roll* and *American Hot Wax*. His most recent hit single was "My Ding-a-Ling" in 1972.

CHUCK BERRY COLLECTORS' GUIDE
—Smash hit in that category

Date	Song	Label	Pop	R&B	C&W
8/55	Maybellene	Chess	•	•	
10/55	Thirty Days	Chess		•	
2/56	No Money Down	Chess		•	
6/56	Roll Over Beethoven	Chess	•	•	
10/56	Too Much Monkey Business/Brown Eyed Handsome Man	Chess		•	
4/57	School Days	Chess		•	
11/57	Rock and Roll Music	Chess	•	•	
2/58	Sweet Little Sixteen	Chess	•	•	
4/58	Johnny B. Goode	Chess	•	•	
8/58	Carol	Chess	•	•	
11/58	Sweet Little Rock and Roll	Chess		•	
11/58	Joe Joe Gun	Chess			

Date	Song	Label	Pop	R&B	C&W
12/58	Run Rudolph Run	Chess			
12/58	Merry Christmas Baby	Chess			
2/59	Anthony Boy	Chess			
4/59	Almost Grown	Chess		°	
4/59	Little Queenie	Chess			
6/59	Back in the USA	Chess		°	
2/60	Let It Rock	Chess			
2/60	Too Pooped to Pop	Chess		°	
3/64	Nadine	Chess	°		
8/64	No Particular Place to Go	Chess	°		
8/72	My Ding-a-Ling	Chess	°		
12/72	Rollin' and Rockin'	Chess			

ALBUMS

Date	Album	Label
8/63	*On Stage*	Chess
6/64	*Greatest Hits*	Chess
12/64	*St. Louis to Liverpool*	Chess
5/67	*Golden Decade*	Chess
10/72	*Golden Decade*	Chess

BO DIDDLEY

Bo Diddley popularized the Chicago rhythm and blues style of rock 'n' roll. Like many Chicago blues singers, he was originally from rural Mississippi. But his music was quite different from Muddy Waters and the other Chicago bar-blues singers. Diddley's songs had a unique feel that combined the rhythm patterns of "shave-and-a-haircut shampoo" with the intensity of a bump and grind shuffle. This syncopated feel probably came from an African drum rhythm.

Bo Diddley combined this primitive beat with a raw vocal and driving guitar work for his first hit in 1955, "Bo Diddley." This song did not get a great deal of air play. It did do much better in record sales, however, with its strong dance appeal. The Bo Diddley feel has been utilized on many other hit records through the years, including Johnny Otis's, "Willie and the Hand Jive" (1957);

Bo Diddley (Billy Vera Collection)

Ronnie Hawkins's "Who Do You Love" (1963); and the Rolling Stones' "Not Fade Away" (1966). Bo Diddley is one of the only performers to be identified with a rhythm pattern rather than with any particular song or record.

Ellas McDaniels was born in McComb, Mississippi, in 1928. When he was very young, his family moved to Chicago. He got his nickname in elementary school and used it later as an amateur boxer. Bo Diddley played the violin before he learned the guitar. His family was so poor that his music teacher took up a church collection to buy the youngster a violin. After several years, he received a guitar as a Christmas present and learned to play it. He was strongly influenced by blues singer John Lee Hooker's recording of "Boogie Children."

In 1949, Bo Diddley began working at the 708 Club on Chicago's tough South Side. In 1955, he auditioned for the Chess brothers with an original song called "Uncle John." They asked him to revise the song. One of the revisions was changing the title to "Bo Diddley."

Bo's records were quite popular among dancers and record buyers, although they did not receive a great deal of air play. His first record, "Bo Diddley," was rated number eight on jukebox plays, but did not make the top twenty-five in disc jockey plays. His raw singing style seemed to go over best at loud parties or in noisy bars. He was a visual performer who projected much more in person than on records. Wearing loud clothing and sporting an unusual shaped guitar, he was always a big favorite at rock 'n' roll shows.

Bo Diddley's second biggest hit, "Say Man," was written spontaneously and recorded in thirty-five takes in 1959. The song had humorous lyrics and the classic Bo Diddley beat. His later records have had only modest success. Bo continues to record for the Chess-Checker Company (All Platinum Records).

After years of playing only the black circuit, Bo has found a new audience with the rock 'n' roll revival. In the fifties, he recalls, his beat was considered too primitive by many black people because it was more closely rooted in African rhythms than the music of other rhythm and blues artists. But to Bo, his unique feel was his claim to originality. Unlike many of his contemporaries in Chicago, Bo Diddley did not try to play traditional blues. Instead, he developed his own sound. Many other performers have successfully copied this style, but the man they must all pay tribute to is Bo Diddley.

BO DIDDLEY COLLECTORS' GUIDE
—Smash hit in that category

Date	Song	Label	Pop	R&B	C&W
5/55	Bo Diddley/I'm A Man	Checker		°	
7/55	Diddley Daddy	Checker		°	
3/59	I'm Sorry	Checker		°	
8/59	Crackin' Up	Checker		°	
9/59	Say Man	Checker		°	
12/59	Say Man, Back Again	Checker			
4/60	Road Runner	Checker		°	
8/62	You Can't Judge a Book by the Cover	Checker			
1/67	Ooh Baby	Checker		°	

ALBUMS

Date	Album	Label
11/62	*Bo Diddley*	Checker

VOCAL GROUP MUSIC

Vocal groups made some of the most important music in the early years of rock 'n' roll. Many of these group hits were slow songs that featured intricate patterns of vocal harmony. The other four styles of rock 'n' roll were based on the various blues forms and depended on an interplay between musical instruments and human voices. The majority of vocal groups, however, used a minimum of instrumentation—just enough to keep a basic beat. This music, which was strongly influenced by gospel singing, used the beauty and variety of vocal blends to get its message across.

The earliest black vocal groups to achieve commercial success in the pop market were the Mills Brothers and the Ink Spots. The latter group, featuring lead singer Bill Kenny and talking bassman

The Orioles ("Bleecker" Bob Plotnik Collection)

"Hoppy" Jones, had a series of hits in the late thirties and early forties. The Ink Spots began to decline in popularity in the mid-forties, but their success encouraged many others.

In 1948, a new group, the Orioles, achieved national renown with their first hit, "It's Too Soon to Know." Their style was somewhat rougher than the Ink Spots and featured more varied background singing. Most of the major record labels ignored the Orioles as just another black group recording "race" music (music geared to the black audience). But many small, independent companies realized that there was money to be made in the R&B market. When the Orioles recorded their second R&B smash, "Tell

The Penguins ("Bleecker" Bob Plotnik Collection)

Me So," in 1949, they hit on a cool and simple style that was to be widely copied in the early fifties.

The Orioles featured the cool but emotional tenor voice of Sonny Til. They represented a new style of black singing and showmanship. The group dressed sharply and moved around the stage in choreographed steps. From 1949 to 1953, the Orioles were the most successful R&B vocal group. When their cover version of the country record "Crying in the Chapel" made the pop charts in 1953, the Orioles had opened the door to a whole new musical era.

Nineteen fifty-four was the year that several records by black vocal groups became big pop hits. These included "Gee" by the Crows, "Earth Angel" by the Penguins, "Sh-Boom" by the Chords, and "Hearts of Stone" by the Charms. These songs would have been even more successful had it not been for the well-promoted white cover versions which, in many cases, outsold the originals. For the most part, rock 'n' roll vocal groups had only one or two hits before disappearing from the music scene. Charlie Gillett believes that the short-lived appeal of most of these groups was caused by their novelty appeal. In many cases, a record sold because of an "oddity" in the song or in the lead singer's style. These oddities, which seemed strange to white listeners, were often familiar sounds to the R&B audience.

Another characteristic of many vocal groups records was the romantic feelings they captured. The lyrics of many of these songs resembled pop ballads more closely than any of the other rock 'n' roll styles. The group sound seemed to express the loneliness and innocence of teenage love. The following are typical lyrics from a vocal group song, "The Closer You Are," recorded by the Channels in 1956:

The Channels
("Bleecker" Bob
Plotnik Collection)

The closer you are, the brighter the stars in the sky,
And darling, I realize, you're the one in my heart.
The closer you are, the brighter the flames in my heart,
And darling we'll never part, we'll always be in love.

When I first saw you, I did adore you, and your loving ways
And then you went away, but now you're back to stay,
And my love for you grows stronger every day.

Although these lyrics are similar to those of many sentimental pop songs, the heavy rock 'n' roll afterbeat and emotional singing of the group give the song a completely different flavor. Many of the devices used by the vocal groups were derived from black gospel music. Thus, many of the songs have a feeling of reverence and humility.

Because of the relative innocence of their sound, black vocal groups were the first R&B performers to gain exposure on television and pop radio stations. Hundreds of independent record companies recorded thousands of aspiring groups who were seeking stardom. For a small amount of money, a producer could take a young group into the studio and record them in a matter of minutes. There are many stories in the music business of young groups that became instant success stories. One such group, Frankie

Frankie Lymon and the Teenagers ("Bleecker" Bob Plotnik Collection)

Lymon and the Teenagers, was one of the few to have a series of hits. Record producer Bobby Robinson tells how he almost signed the group:

> A friend of mine, Richard Barrett, told me that there was this little group up at P.S. 165 in Harlem with a dynamite lead singer. "Let me bring them down to your place tomorrow after school for just five minutes," he said. "They do a number, 'Why Do Fools Fall in Love,' that makes the kids go wild." I told him to bring them down, but unfortunately, I got detained and was about fifteen minutes late. Well, I guess the kids were getting restless, so Richard took them downtown to another producer, George Goldner. He just hired a few musicians and had the group do the song just like they had been doing it in the school auditorium. The record was completed that same night and became a huge hit. That's how I missed signing Frankie Lymon by fifteen minutes, although I did sign and record his younger brother Louie.

The success of boy-soprano Frankie Lymon and his group fired the hopes of young singers in urban ghettos all over the country. A small percentage of these groups managed to make one record that sold. The great majority, however, never even got to hear their records on the radio.

Fifties vocal groups are often called "doo-wop" groups, because those syllables were often used by the bass singer in an attempt to imitate the rhythmic sound of a string bass. There were, of course, many other nonsense sounds used by these singers like, "dum-ba, dum-ba," "hubba, hubba, hubba, hubba," "wop, wah-ooh," and many others. The bass singer in these doo-wop groups was usually second in importance to the lead tenor. These low end voices provided rhythmic emphasis in some cases and stuttering humor in others.

The lead voices in doo-wop groups were of two broad types—the cool, detached style, popularized by the Orioles' Sonny Til, and the dramatic emotional style, used with great success by Tony Williams of the Platters. In between these two extremes, lead singers used varying degrees of emotion. There were also differences in the amount of vocal support given by the rest of the group. Gillett feels that the amount of group support depended on the strength of the lead singer. For example, the Platters used sparse and unimaginative vocal support behind the powerful voice of Williams. On the other hand, a group with a weak lead singer would often use stronger and more complex background singing. There are many exceptions to this formula. Many of the best doo-wop records featured both strong leads and excellent group support.

Although most people associate the doo-wop groups with slow, romantic songs, there were a comparable number of up-tempo hits. Some of the more memorable ones were "Ling Ting Tong," by the Charms (1954); "Speedo," by the Cadillacs (1955); "I Want You to Be My Girl," by Frankie Lymon and the Teenagers (1956); "Whispering Bells," by the Del Vikings (1957); and "Book of Love," by the Monotones (1958). These fast songs almost always featured a tenor sax solo about halfway through the record. In general, groups tried to couple a fast side with a slow side. Still, it was difficult to vary the sound and the lyrics within these two styles.

While fast vocal group songs were often humorous novelty numbers, slow doo-wop records were almost always concerned with love. In some cases, the lyrics were a plea for affection ("Earth Angel" by the Penguins; "Please Say You Want Me" by the Schoolboys). At other times, singers longed for their departed lovers ("Story Untold" by the Nutmegs; "Tears on My Pillow" by Little Anthony and the Imperials). A third type of vocal group love songs spoke of the joys of togetherness ("In the Still of the

The Cadillacs ("Bleecker" Bob Plotnik Collection)

The Del Vikings ("Bleecker" Bob Plotnik Collection)

Night" by the Five Satins; "Oh What a Night" by the Dells). For the most part, these slow songs were similar in both instrumentation and musical structure. The uniqueness of a particular record usually depended on the delivery of the lead singer, although a few group hits are remembered more for their creative background singing.

There were several important recordings by solo singers and duos that were closer to the vocal group style than to any other kind of rock 'n' roll. One of these records, "Pledging My Love," by Johnny Ace, was among the most important early rock 'n' roll hits. Ace was an enormously popular R&B performer in the early fifties. Before he became a solo singer, Ace was the piano player in the Beale Streeters band in Memphis. This group also included guitar player B. B. King and singer Bobby "Blue" Bland. Ace was essentially a ballad singer with a rather plaintive voice.

"Pledging My Love" had no background singers, and a rather smooth beat for a rock 'n' roll song. The featured instrument was a vibraphone, and Ace's singing was somewhat sentimental for an R&B performer. Nevertheless, the record is one of the most popular and beloved slow oldies. Its influence is reflected in such rock 'n' roll ballad style hits as "Tear Drops" and "Long Lonely Nights," both recorded by Lee Andrews and the Hearts in 1957.

Little Anthony and the Imperials ("Bleecker" Bob Plotnik Collection)

Vocal duos had their own distinct sound in the fifties. Both singers usually sang the material in close harmony, although call and response and other vocal techniques were sometimes heard. The two most memorable records in this style were "Over the Mountain, Across the Sea" by Johnnie and Joe (1957) and "We Belong Together" by Robert and Johnny (1958). Both of these records expressed the yearnings and emotions of young love. This approach proved commercially successful again in 1962 with Don and Juan's "What's Your Name?" Like most of the doo-wop groups, the vocal duos could not follow up their one hit record.

Out of the thousands of groups to make a record in the middle and late fifties, only three were able to maintain successful recording careers over several years: the Platters, the Coasters, and the Drifters. Dozens of other groups had one or two important records. These are listed in the Collectors' Guide, or in the sections on the years that they were popular.

VOCAL GROUPS COLLECTORS' GUIDE

Year	Song	Artist	Label
1956	A Thousand Miles Away	The Heartbeats	Rama
1956	Can't We Be Sweethearts	The Cleftones	Gee
1957	Could This Be Magic	The Dubs	Gone
1957	Don't Ask Me to Be Lonely	The Dubs	Gone
1958	For Your Precious Love	Jerry Butler and The Impressions	Abner
1956	I'll Be Home	The Flamingos	Checker
1958	One Summer Night	The Danleers	Mercury
1956	Oh What a Night	The Dells	Vee Jay
1958	Over the Mountain	Johnnie and Joe	Chess
1958	Ten Commandments of Love	The Moonglows	Chess
1957	Tonite Tonite	The Mello Kings	Herald
1955	Story Untold	The Nutmegs	Herald
1958	You Cheated	The Shields	Tender
1956	I Promise to Remember	Frankie Lymon and the Teenagers	Gee

THE PLATTERS

The Platters, with sixteen gold records between 1955 and 1960, were the most popular vocal group of that era. Most of the other vocal groups who had early rock 'n' roll hits never became successfully established in the pop market. One of the earliest big hits by a black singing group was the Penguins' "Earth Angel" on the Dootone Label in 1954. The group was managed by songwriter Buck Ram. When Mercury Records bought the Penguins' contract, Ram insisted that they also sign another one of his groups, the Platters. Ram had written "Only You," which the Platters first recorded on the Federal label. After the group signed with Mercury, the song was recut and became the first of four number one records for the group.

The Platters originally consisted of four men—Tony Williams, Dave Lynch, Paul Robi, and Herb Reed. While the group was in its early years with Federal, Ram recruited Zola Taylor, a fifteen-year-old girl, in order to give the group a unique sound. As it turned out, Zola only gave the group a unique look. The sound of the group came almost exclusively from the emotional voice of lead singer Tony Williams.

"Only You" was similar to many sentimental ballads which white crooners had been recording for twenty years, but the Platters' rendering of the song was authentic rock 'n' roll. While the group sustained relaxed chords over an easy rock 'n' roll beat, Williams's emotional lead tenor soared dramatically.

The Platters' second release on Mercury was another Buck Ram composition, "The Great Pretender." It was the group's best and biggest selling record. The song uses the classic love-story theme

The Platters ("Bleecker" Bob Plotnik Collection)

of the clown who is laughing on the outside while crying on the inside. The theatrical qualities of Williams's voice are fully realized, while in the musical spaces, the group sadly moaned, "Ooh, ooh, ooh, ooh."

The Platters continued to record hits in their slow style. Every song contained sentimental lyrics which were dramatically sung by Williams. Some of their material was old standards like "My Prayer" and "Twilight Time." These were recorded in pretty much the same style as Ram's songs. The group had attracted a wide audience that included adults as well as teens, blacks as well as whites.

Because the Platters combined white and black styles in their music, they received criticism as well as adulation from both audiences. Many blacks and rock 'n' roll purists considered the Platters' sound too white to be authentic. Yet many of the group's biggest pop hits found their way to the top ten of the rhythm and blues charts. At the same time, some conservative white listeners felt the group's sound was too black for the pop market.

After 1958 the group's popularity began to decline. By this time, they were recording old standards almost exclusively. Their records became increasingly sentimental and predictable. Lacking an exciting piece of original material, the group seemed to lose their magic.

The downfall of the Platters came in 1960 when Williams left the group. Although his voice was the mainstay of all Platters' records, Williams could not make it as a solo performer. Sonny Turner replaced Williams as the group's lead singer, but the Platters never had another hit record.

Today Tony Williams lives in New York City. Together with his wife Helen, his son, and two new members, he is working the revival circuit as Tony Williams and the Platters.

THE PLATTERS COLLECTORS' GUIDE
—Smash hit in that category

Date	Song	Label	Pop	R&B	C&W
9/55	Only You	Mercury	*	*	
11/55	The Great Pretender	Mercury	*	*	
2/56	I'm Just a Dancing Partner	Mercury			
3/56	(You've Got) the Magic Touch	Mercury	*	*	

Date	Song	Label	Pop	R&B	C&W
3/56	Winner Take All	Mercury			
6/56	My Prayer	Mercury	*	*	
7/56	Heaven on Earth	Mercury			
9/56	You'll Never Never Know	Mercury	*	*	
9/56	It Isn't Right	Mercury		*	
12/56	On My Word of Honor	Mercury		*	
12/56	One in a Million	Mercury		*	
3/57	I'm Sorry	Mercury	*		
3/57	He's Mine	Mercury			
5/57	My Dream	Mercury		*	
5/57	Only Because	Mercury			
10/57	Helpless	Mercury			
3/58	Twilight Time	Mercury	*	*	
6/58	You're Making a Mistake	Mercury			
9/58	I Wish	Mercury			
10/58	It's Raining Outside	Mercury			
11/58	Smoke Gets in Your Eyes	Mercury	*	*	
4/59	Enchanted	Mercury	*	*	
6/59	Remember When	Mercury			
9/59	Where	Mercury			
9/59	Wish It Were Me	Mercury			
1/60	Harbor Lights	Mercury	*	*	
2/60	Sleepy Lagoon	Mercury			
5/60	Ebb Tide	Mercury			
8/60	Red Sails in the Sunset	Mercury			
10/60	To Each His Own	Mercury			
1/61	If I Didn't Care	Mercury			
4/61	Trees	Mercury			
8/61	I'll Never Smile Again	Mercury		*	
2/62	It's Magic	Mercury			
2/67	With This Ring	Mercury	*	*	

ALBUMS

Date	Album	Label
7/14/56	*The Platters*	Mercury
1/9/57	*The Platters*—Volume 2	Mercury
3/21/59	*Remember When*	Mercury
3/14/60	*Encore of Golden Hits*	Mercury
11/13/60	*More Encore of Golden Hits*	Mercury

THE DRIFTERS

The Drifters were originally formed by Clyde McPhatter after he left the Dominoes. As lead singer for the Dominoes, Clyde's voice had been featured on rhythm and blues hits like "Do Something for Me" and "Have Mercy Baby." When he left the Dominoes in 1953, McPhatter got together with several members of a gospel group called the Clivetones. He called this new combination the Drifters, because each member had drifted from one group to another.

The Dominoes with Clyde McPhatter ("Bleecker" Bob Plotnik Collection)

The Drifters ("Bleecker" Bob Plotnik Collection)

The Drifters' first release for Atlantic Records in September 1954, "Money Honey," was a rhythm and blues hit. Several follow-up records were also well received by the rhythm and blues audience including "Bip Bam," "Honey Love" (written by McPhatter), and Irving Berlin's "White Christmas." In 1954, McPhatter left the group to become a solo artist.

During the next four years, the Drifters went through a succession of personnel changes. They made some good but relatively unheard-of records, including the much acclaimed "I Gotta Get Myself a Woman" in 1956.

By the summer of 1958, the group had disbanded. But George Treadwell, who managed the Drifters, had signed contracts for the group to perform at the Apollo Theater in Harlem in New York City. In an attempt to honor his commitments, Treadwell convinced another group, the Five Crowns, to perform and record under the Drifters' name. It was this group, featuring Ben E. King singing lead, that began having mass market hits in 1959.

The first hit record of the new Drifters was "There Goes My Baby," a song written by King and Treadwell. Producers Jerry Leiber and Mike Stoller decided to experiment with this loosely structured song. They combined the high gospel sound of King's voice with a low string section that played moving lines that resembled rhythm and blues horn riffs. This new combination of sounds proved an artistic and commercial success. "There Goes My Baby" made the top ten and was one of the year's best records.

Leiber and Stoller's pioneering use of strings with the Drifters was copied by many other producers. To be sure, it required great skill to use strings in an effective and understated way on rock 'n' roll records. In many cases, the strings became too lush. They tended to soften the impact of the singers and rhythm instruments. Indeed, Leiber and Stoller had difficulty achieving a correct balance on the Drifters' next records. "Dance with Me" (1959), "This Magic Moment" (1960), and "Save the Last Dance for Me" (1960) were all top ten hits. But compared with "There Goes My Baby," these later records sounded more conventional and less exciting. King was now singing in a lower voice, and without gospel inflections. The string arrangements were higher and more lush sounding, and a Latin rhumba beat softened the sound even more.

In 1960, Ben E. King left the Drifters to pursue a solo career. His first record, "Spanish Harlem," was a big hit. It was co-written and produced by Phil Spector. King had several follow-up hits "Stand By Me" (1961), "Don't Play That Song" (1962), and "I Who Have Nothing" (1963).

After the departure of King, Rudy Lewis became the group's lead singer. Lewis's style strongly resembled the early singing of King. The Drifters had a series of hits between 1962 and 1964 with lyrics that concerned life in the city. These included, "Up on the

Roof," written by Carole King and Gerry Coffin; "On Broadway," which was revived by George Benson in 1977; and the melodic, "Under the Boardwalk," re-recorded by the Rolling Stones.

When George Treadwell died in 1967, his wife Faye took over the management of the group. Clyde McPhatter and Rudy Lewis have both passed away. Ben E. King still works as a solo performer. There are currently no less than three groups performing as the Drifters in various revival shows.

THE DRIFTERS COLLECTORS' GUIDE
—Smash hit in that category

Date	Song	Label	Pop	R&B	C&W
10/53	Money Honey	Atlantic		*	
3/54	Such a Night	Atlantic		*	
3/54	Lucille	Atlantic		*	
6/54	Honey Love	Atlantic		*	
11/54	Bip Bam	Atlantic		*	
12/54	White Christmas	Atlantic		*	
3/55	Whatcha Gonna Do	Atlantic		*	
11/55	Adorable/Steamboat	Atlantic		*	
5/55	Ruby Baby	Atlantic		*	
8/56	I Gotta Get Myself a Woman	Atlantic			
2/57	Fools Fall in Love	Atlantic			
6/57	Hypnotized	Atlantic			
6/58	Moonlight Bay	Atlantic			
8/58	Drip Drop	Atlantic			
6/59	There Goes My Baby	Atlantic	*	*	
10/59	Dance with Me	Atlantic	*		
11/59	True Love, True Love	Atlantic			
2/60	This Magic Moment	Atlantic	*	*	
5/60	Lonely Winds	Atlantic			
9/60	Save the Last Dance for Me	Atlantic	*	*	
12/60	I Count the Tears	Atlantic	*		
3/61	Some Kind of Wonderful	Atlantic	*		
5/61	Please Stay	Atlantic			
10/61	Sweets for the Sweet	Atlantic	*		
12/61	Roomful of Tears	Atlantic			
2/62	When My Little Girl Is Smiling	Atlantic	*		
5/62	Strangers on the Shore	Atlantic			
11/62	Up on the Roof	Atlantic	*	*	
3/63	On Broadway	Atlantic	*		

Date	Song	Label	Pop	R&B	C&W
5/63	Rat Race	Atlantic			
8/63	I'll Take You Home	Atlantic			
5/64	Under the Boardwalk	Atlantic	°		
11/64	Saturday Night at the Movies	Atlantic	°		

ALBUMS

Date	Album	Label
6/8/63	*Up on the Roof*	Atlantic
3/16/68	*The Drifters Golden Hits*	Atlantic

THE COASTERS

The Coasters were one of the most successful and interesting vocal groups of the fifties. The group, originally called the Robins, first recorded for Spark Records, which was owned by producers-songwriters Jerry Leiber and Mike Stoller. Generally considered to be among the very best writers of early rock 'n' roll, Leiber and Stoller wrote many classic songs, including "Hound Dog" and "Kansas City." The two had cut a song called "Smokey Joe's Cafe" with the Robins in 1955. The record got some notice on the West Coast rhythm and blues charts and came to the attention of Atlantic Records' president Ahmet Ertegun. The New York company not only signed the Robins, they signed Leiber and Stoller as independent producers. At this point, the group underwent several personnel changes and became known as the Coasters.

After several relatively unnoticed releases in 1956, the group struck gold. "Searchin'/Young Blood" was a huge two-sided hit in 1957. "Searchin', " the bigger pop hit of the two, told of a lover's attempt to find his girl. Sung in a raw but humorous style by baritone Billy Guy, the singer swore to use the methods of famous detectives like Charlie Chan, Sergeant Friday, and Bulldog Drummond to track down his lost love. The song set the pattern for the group's humorous but soulful sound. "Searchin' " was one of the first songs to mention well-known fictional characters in its lyrics. This approach was used on several other successful records, such as "Western Movies" by the Olympics in 1958 and "Ally Oop" by the Hollywood Argyles in 1960.

On "Young Blood," the B side of "Searchin'," the group created the feeling of a bunch of guys hanging out on a street corner checking out the girls who walked by. A technique used in this song was a break in the music during which bass singer Dub Jones delivered the comic punch line. On some of the breaks each member of the group would echo the same line like "Looka there" and "What's your name." Dub Jones played the menacing father who warned the lecherous crowd to leave his daughter alone.

The Coasters followed up their first smash with a series of hit records. "Yakety Yak," released in early 1958, was a clever piece of humorous social commentary and one of the best records of the year. The song staged a drama between a lazy, put-upon youth and his threatening parent. The flip side of "Yakety Yak" was the

The Coasters (Billy Vera Collection)

old standard, "Zing Went the Strings of My Heart." Leiber and Stoller creatively used Dub Jones's bass voice against a slow beat and sustained harmonies by the rest of the group. The resulting sound was interesting and strangely moving.

In 1959, "Charlie Brown" became the group's third top ten hit. The main character of this song was the class goof-off and trouble-maker. Although he is always getting in trouble, he keeps asking why everyone is always picking on him. Like many Coasters' hits, this record featured the innovative saxophone sound of King Curtis. The stuttering or "yakety" sax sound that Curtis developed became an important part of the Coasters' music.

Among the group's other hits, "Poison Ivy" and "Along Came Jones" were the most important. "Poison Ivy," a girl to look at but not touch, had a similar vocal flavor to "Searchin'. " "Along Came Jones" was a spoof on television's western heros that used some of the comic techniques of "Young Blood." "Little Egypt," released in 1961, was a Coasters' record that had less success.

Leiber and Stoller, who wrote most of the group's material, were able to combine social commentary and comedy with an authentic rock 'n' roll sound. Their records with the Coasters expressed teenage concerns in a humorous and sympathetic way that is unmatched in the history of rock 'n' roll.

The Coasters have gone through various personnel changes in the sixties and seventies. There are currently at least two versions of the Coasters working the revival circuit. The current group (or groups) emphasize funny stage routines in order to maintain their image as the foremost comedy-vocal group of rock 'n' roll.

THE COASTERS COLLECTORS' GUIDE
*—Smash hit in that category

Date	Song	Label	Pop	R&B	C&W
3/56	Down in Mexico	Atco		°	
9/56	One Kiss Led to Another	Atco			
5/57	Searchin'	Atco	°	°	
5/57	Young Blood	Atco	°	°	
10/57	Idol with the Golden Head	Atco			
5/58	Yakety Yak	Atco	°	°	
2/59	Charlie Brown	Atco	°	°	
7/59	Along Came Jones	Atco	°	°	
8/59	Poison Ivy	Atco	°	°	

Date	Song	Label	Pop	R&B	C&W
9/59	I'm a Hog for You	Atco			
12/59	Run Red Run	Atco			
12/59	What About Us	Atco			
12/59	Besame Mucho	Atco			
6/60	Wake Me, Shake Me	Atco		°	
10/60	Shoppin' for Clothes	Atco			
2/61	Wait a Minute	Atco		°	
4/61	Little Egypt	Atco		°	
8/61	Girls Girls Girls	Atco			
12/71	Love Potion #9	King			

FEMALE VOCAL GROUPS

The music made by female vocal groups in the late fifties and early sixties was both appealing and memorable. Although many of the records by these so-called girl groups used familiar rhythm and blues devices, the music had a feeling all its own. Of the four female groups that had hit records before 1958, only the Chantels were able to follow up their initial success. The group featured the powerful voice of Arlene Smith, whom many consider one of the greatest female singers in the history of rock 'n' roll. She had an emotional sound that was used to great effect on pleading love songs like "Maybe," "He's Gone," and "I Love You So." Although the Chantels disbanded in the early sixties, they influenced the many successful female vocal groups that followed.

The Shirelles were the first group to have hits in a style that was to be widely copied by many of the girl groups in the early sixties. While lead singer Shirley Alston sang in an appealing little-girl style, the rest of the group sang rhythmic background harmonies. Their sound was cute but tough. In contrast to the Chantels' heartfelt pleas, the Shirelles freely offered their affections to the right boy. In songs like "Baby It's You," "Tonight's the Night," and "Will You Still Love Me Tomorrow," the group established the sound and attitude that characterized the girl group style. The Shirelles had a series of hits of this type from 1958 to 1963 and were the most successful female vocal group during this period.

The Chantels ("Bleecker" Bob Plotnik Collection)

The success of the Shirelles encouraged record companies to record dozens of other girl groups. The songs that these groups sang were usually written by professional songwriters who were not part of the group. Many of these writers worked out of publishing companies located in the Brill Building in New York. One of them was Carole King, who co-wrote "Will You Still Love Me

Tomorrow" for the Shirelles and "The Locomotion" for Little Eva. Other writers of this era were Neil Sedaka and the team of Doc Pomus and Mort Shuman. But the most successful writers of girl group hits were Jeff Barry and Ellie Greewich, who often wrote with Phil Spector.

Once a song was written for a particular group, the producer had almost complete control over the record-making process. The music that resulted was among the most carefully planned of all rock 'n' roll. This approach was perfected by Spector, considered to be the major figure of early sixties rock 'n' roll. Spector added large orchestras to the tough sound of the girl groups. The music that came out was dense and powerful. His best records are rock 'n' roll classics that sound just as good today as they did fifteen years ago. These gems include the Crystals' "He's a Rebel" and "Then He Kissed Me," and Bob B. Soxx and the Blue Jeans' "Why Do Lovers Break Each Other's Heart" and "Zip-a-Dee-Doo Dah."

The importance of the producer cannot be denied in the making of the girl group sound. It is clear that the producers had more

The Shirelles at a recent club date with guitarist Billy Vera (Billy Vera Collection)

The Crystals (Billy Vera Collection)

creative control than the performers. The girl singers did manage to project their personalities onto their records. From the little girl styles of the Shirelles and the Crystals to the street-tough sounds of the Ronettes, female vocal groups expressed a wide range of feelings. But the importance of the producers on these records is supported by the lack of individual success by most of the great

The Ronettes (Billy Vera Collection)

The Chiffons (Billy Vera Collection)

female lead singers. Once a group split with its original producer, it rarely made another hit record.

The girl group sound captured many teenage attitudes in the late fifties and early sixties. Many of the records, like the Orlons' "Wah Watusi" and the Marvellettes' "Twistin' Postman," were geared to current dance crazes. Many other records featured the boy as the star of the story. Songs like "He's a Rebel" by the Crystals and "Leader of the Pack" by the Shangri-Las idealized the tough male teenager. Some songs were concerned with a handsome and lovable boy, like "He's So Fine" by the Chiffons. Still, another type of song like the Marvellettes' "Playboy" warned girls to watch out for certain types of boys. Whether he is the protective type, as in the Angels' "My Boyfriend's Back," or cruel, as in the Crystals' "He Hit Me," the boy is at the center of most girl group records.

The era of the female vocal group passed in the mid-sixties. Many of the performers are no longer in the music business. Some groups like the Shirelles work regularly at oldies shows, but no longer make hit records. Although most of the groups have disbanded, the spirit of their music lives on. The black female sound certainly influenced the early Beatles. They even re-recorded a Marvellettes' hit as "Please Mr. Postman" on an early album. Later in their career, the Beatles used Phil Spector as a producer in an attempt to recapture some of the magic of his early productions. Contemporary artists like Bruce Springsteen borrowed musical ideas from girl group records and tried to reconstruct Spector's "wall of sound."

FEMALE GROUPS COLLECTORS' GUIDE

Year	Song	Artist	Label
1958	Down the Aisle of Love	The Quintones	Hunt
1962	He's Sure the Boy I Love	The Crystals	Philles
1958	I Love You So	The Chantels	End
1961	Look in My Eyes	The Chantels	End
1958	I Met Him on a Sunday	The Shirelles	Scepter
1960	Tonight's the Night	The Shirelles	Scepter
1960	Will You Still Love Me Tomorrow	The Shirelles	Scepter
1962	Chains	The Cookies	Dimension
1963	The Kind of Boy You Can't Forget	The Raindrops	Jubilee
1962	Tell Him	The Exciters	United Artists

ROCK 'N' SOUL

The popularity of the new rock 'n' roll styles affected both the pop and rhythm and blues markets. By the late fifties, white teenagers showed a growing interest in the music of black artists.

Jackie Wilson (Neal Hollander Collection)

Gospel-influenced records like "Shout" by the Isley Brothers and "Lonely Teardrops" by Jackie Wilson did well on the pop charts. Another enormously popular record which was rooted in black church music was Ray Charles's "What'd I Say." This song managed to combine the feeling of a gospel sermon with the lyrics and beat of rock 'n' roll. "What'd I Say" became a rock 'n' roll standard that was recorded by Elvis Presley and many other performers. The success of Ray Charles, Jackie Wilson, and the Isleys in 1959 showed that there was a large audience with an interest in gospel-flavored R&B. At the same time, many black artists were trying to gear their sound to the pop audience. One of the first to succeed was the late Sam Cooke.

In 1957, Sam Cooke left the Soul Stirrers, a well-loved gospel group, to begin a career as a pop singer. Compared to the high voltage gospel stylings of Ray Charles, Cooke's records sounded tame. Many of his hits featured polished studio arrangements and innocent lyrics, but Cooke managed to keep his original singing style intact. Unlike most of the shouting type gospel singers, Cooke had a soft and sexy voice which made the girls sigh. Writer Arnold Shaw has gone so far as to compare Sam's appeal to that of

The Isley Brothers (Neal Hollander Collection)

Frank Sinatra. But producers like Motown's Berry Gordy understood that the pop-gospel sound was to be an important trend in the future of popular music. Between the frantic shouting and preaching of Ray Charles's "What'd I Say" and the smooth sound of Sam Cooke's "You Send Me" was a new musical territory which came to be known as "soul music."

Just as Elvis's early records broke down the barriers between R&B and country music, the early soul hits helped to bring several kinds of black music together. By the mid-sixties, the sounds of gospel music, blues, and pop had been successfully combined.

RAY CHARLES

Ray Charles was born in Albany, Georgia, in 1930, but moved to Greenville, Florida, as a young child. At age six, he developed an illness that left him completely blind. Ray learned Braille and began playing the piano as a teenager. By the time he was fifteen, Ray's parents had both passed away. Shortly thereafter, he organized his own trio and took to the road. He began recording in 1951, with a sound reminiscent to black pop singer Nat King Cole. Several years later, Ray changed his style and emerged as perhaps the most important figure in popular music during the last twenty-five years.

Ray Charles—"The high priest of soul" (Courtesy of *Record World* magazine)

Also known as "the Reverend" and "the genius," Ray Charles has been a pioneer in jazz as well as contemporary popular music. Aside from being one of the most influential singers and musicians of this era, Ray almost single-handedly invented several new styles of music. Because the range of his concept was so great, Charles was not afraid to combine various styles in order to achieve a desired result. His early records on Atlantic used gospel forms to express concerns most commonly associated with blues singing. These two musical styles—gospel and blues—had been considered as separate as a church and a barroom by most God-fearing black people. Charles, however, recognized that the two forms were very much alike. The musical structure and intensity of both gospel and blues music were derived, after all, from the same cultural heritage. By the mid-fifties Charles had joined these styles in songs like "Drown in My Own Tears," "Hallelujah I Love Her So," and "I Got a Woman." Ray simply took a traditional melody from the black church, changed the lyrics, and preached a new kind of gospel.

Charles's gospel-blues records maintained the excitement and frenzy of church singing, but the words were not religious in the usual sense. In "I Got a Woman" and "Hallelujah I Love Her So," the singer is celebrating his love. He is saying that in this troubled world, he can turn to his woman and she will make him feel great joy. In the live version of "Drown in My Own Tears," Charles uses an almost painfully slow gospel structure to sing about a familiar blues theme, lost love. He masterfully employs the call and response technique with his background singers (the Raylettes) and his audience.

Although Ray was recognized as an important jazz musician and rhythm and blues artist, he did not make a real impact on the pop market until 1959. His early records were even rejected by Alan Freed and other disc jockeys who seemed to favor black artists. But in 1959, Ray's gospel style reached the mass market. "What'd I Say," a Charles original, began with a perpetual figure from the bass guitar and picked up steam from Ray's rolling gospel-style piano. By the end of the song, the band and singers had reached a fever pitch that was outdistanced only by Charles's frantic vocal. "What'd I Say" was widely covered and seemed to open the door for other gospel-influenced records.

At the same time the mass audience began discovering him, Ray was also making his impact in jazz. Recording some of his sides with such well-known jazz musicians as Milt Jackson of the Modern Jazz Quartet, Charles incorporated a basic blues and gospel flavor in his jazz records. This combination led to a new musical style called "funk." Many of Charles's Atlantic albums contained both rhythm and blues as well as jazz cuts. No other artist has ever moved so gracefully from one musical style to another.

In 1960, Ray moved to the ABC-Paramount label and cut several records which closely resembled his work at Atlantic. One of the best was the clever "Hit the Road Jack," which used a call and response style similar to "What'd I Say." In 1961, Ray collaborated with jazz arranger Quincy Jones on an album, *Genius Plus Soul Equals Jazz.* The results were interesting and generated the instrumental hit single, "One Mint Julep," which featured Ray's funky organ playing.

Another of Charles's many musical styles, which characterized his early years at ABC, were ballads featuring strings and choral singing. The best of these records was "Georgia on My Mind" which was a smash in 1960–1961. In 1962 Ray recorded an album of country standards that included "Born to Lose" and "Your Cheating Heart." His biggest hit in this style was "I Can't Stop Loving You."

Ray had several good records in the mid-sixties, including the rollicking "Let's Go Get Stoned." But in general his work began to lose some of its early spark. His later records include covers of the Beatles' "Yesterday" and "Eleanor Rigby."

Today, Charles still performs at concerts all over the country and is often seen on television. His music has affected almost every performer in the field of popular music.

RAY CHARLES COLLECTORS' GUIDE
—Smash hit in that category

Date	Song	Label	Pop	R&B	C&W
3/51	Baby Let Me Hold Your Hand	Swing Time		•	
3/52	Kiss Me Baby	Swing Time		•	
3/54	It Should've Been Me	Atlantic		•	
8/54	Don't You Know	Atlantic		•	

Date	Song	Label	Pop	R&B	C&W
1/55	I've Got a Woman/Come Back	Atlantic		✲	
6/55	A Fool for You/This Little Girl of Mine	Atlantic		✲	
10/55	Blackjack/Greenbacks	Atlantic		✲	
2/56	Drown in My Own Tears	Atlantic		✲	
6/56	Hallelujah I Love Her So	Atlantic		✲	
10/56	Lonely Avenue	Atlantic		✲	
2/57	Ain't That Love	Atlantic		✲	
10/57	Swanee River Rock	Atlantic		✲	
12/58	Rockhouse Part 2	Atlantic		✲	
2/59	The Right Time	Atlantic		✲	
4/59	That's Enough	Atlantic		✲	
7/59	What'd I Say	Atlantic	✲	✲	
11/59	I'm Moving On	Atlantic		✲	
1/60	Let the Good Times Roll	Atlantic			
/60	Don't Let the Sun Catch You Crying	Atlantic		✲	
/60	Just for a Thrill	Atlantic		✲	
6/60	Sticks and Stones	ABC		✲	
/60	Tell the Truth	Atlantic		✲	
10/60	Georgia on My Mind	ABC	✲	✲	
11/60	Ruby	ABC		✲	
12/60	Come Rain or Shine	Atlantic			
1/61	Them That Got	ABC		✲	
2/61	One Mint Julep	Impulse	✲	✲	
6/61	I've Got News for You	Impulse		✲	
9/61	Hit the Road Jack	ABC	✲	✲	
12/61	Unchain My Heart	ABC	✲	✲	
2/62	Baby It's Cold Outside	ABC			
4/62	Hide Nor Hair/At the Club	ABC	✲	✲	
5/62	I Can't Stop Loving You	ABC	✲	✲	
5/62	Born to Lose	ABC	✲	✲	
10/62	You Are My Sunshine	ABC	✲	✲	
10/62	Your Cheating Heart	ABC	✲	✲	
2/63	Don't Set Me Free	ABC	✲	✲	
4/63	Take These Chains from My Heart	ABC	✲	✲	
6/63	No One/Without Love There Is Nothing	ABC		✲	
9/63	Busted/That Lucky Old Sun	ABC	✲	✲	
12/64	Making Whoopie	ABC		✲	
12/65	Crying Time	ABC	✲	✲	
3/66	Together Again	ABC	✲	✲	
5/66	Let's Go Get Stoned	ABC		✲	

Date	Song	Label	Pop	R&B	C&W
5/67	Here We Go Again	ABC	°	°	
11/67	Yesterday	ABC		°	
6/68	Eleanor Rigby	ABC		°	
7/72	Look What They've Done to My Song Ma	ABC/TRC		°	

ALBUMS

Date	Album	Label
2/19/60	*The Genius of Ray Charles*	Atlantic
7/24/60	*Ray Charles in Person*	Atlantic
9/3/61	*What'd I Say*	Atlantic
8/18/62	*Ray Charles Greatest Hits*	ABC Paramount

SAM COOKE

Sam Cooke, the son of a Baptist minister, was a well-known gospel singer before he ever made a popular record. One of eight children, Sam began singing in his father's Chicago church when he was very young. While in high school, Sam and his brother joined a gospel group called the Highway QC's. During the early fifties, Sam began singing with a well-known gospel group, the Soul Stirrers. Though he was only seventeen, Sam began taking over the lead on a large portion of the group's tunes. His smooth but intense voice was highlighted on such songs as "Pilgrim of Sorrow" and "Touch the Hem of His Garment." Many knowledgeable listeners consider these gospel performances the best of his career.

Sam had recorded several pop songs for Specialty, including "Forever" and "I'll Come Running Back to You." Unfortunately, Art Rupe, the label's owner, did not adequately promote these records. Rupe felt that Cooke's smooth style would not make an impact on the pop market. At the same time, he feared that the Soul Stirrers' audience would be alienated by Cooke's pop records. Bumps Blackwell, who produced Cooke's first pop sides, managed

The Soul Stirrers with Sam Cooke (*bottom center*) (Billy Vera Collection)

to buy out both Sam's contract and his own from Specialty. The two then signed with Keen, another small West Coast label.

Sam's first release for Keen in 1957, "You Send Me," sold over two million records. Written by Sam and his brother L. C., the song introduced the public to a voice that was unlike any that they had ever heard. Cooke had a delicate but intense voice. His clear diction and timbre reminded some people of Nat King Cole. But Cooke had a depth of emotion below his polish which Cole could not touch. Sam had several other hits on Keen between 1957 and 1959. Some of these were trivial songs such as "Everybody Likes to Cha-Cha-Cha," but all of them were elevated by Sam's original and personal vocal style.

Sam Cooke (Courtesy of *Record World* magazine)

In 1960, Cooke moved to RCA, where he had a number of hits that resembled his records on Keen. The biggest of these was "Chain Gang" in 1960. Sam recorded several Twist songs to capitalize on a hot trend in 1962. He managed to impose his authentic style on records like "Havin' a Party" and "Twistin' the Night Away."

Although he recorded many songs that were designed to suit popular tastes, Cooke also wrote and recorded several authentic gospel-blues songs. One of these was the B side of "Havin' a Party." "Bring It on Home to Me," which became a hit in its own right, was built around a familiar phrase in black culture. Cooke managed to retain the original meaning of the phrase while giving it a new setting. The song used a call and response singing style between Cooke and Lou Rawls (originally a gospel singer and later a pop-soul singer on Capitol Records). Another song in which Cooke took a familiar black expression and gave it social and political overtones was on one of his last records, "A Change Is Gonna Come."

Aside from his successful career as a singer and songwriter, Sam also cut some good records as a producer on his own label, Sar. Most of these records were gospel-influenced, and they showed how well Sam understood the uses of gospel music in popular songs. The best known of his productions was "Soothe Me" by the Sims Twins, which made the rhythm and blues top ten in 1961.

Other notable records on Sar were "Lookin' for a Love" by the Valentinos and "Rome Wasn't Built in a Day" by Johnny Taylor.

Like many rock 'n' roll stars, Sam Cooke met an early and tragic death. At the age of twenty-nine he was killed in a shooting incident at a Los Angeles motel. He is remembered as one of the greatest singers in the history of rock 'n' roll.

Another great singer who met an early death, Otis Redding, paid tribute to Sam by recording one of his songs, "Shake." Redding considered Sam to be one of his greatest influences. Many other performers have had commercial success re-recording Cooke's songs in recent years—"Bring It on Home to Me," the Animals; "Another Saturday Night," Cat Stevens; "Wonderful World," Art Garfunkel; and "Only Sixteen," Dr. Hook.

SAM COOKE COLLECTORS' GUIDE
*—Smash hit in that category

Date	Song	Label	Pop	R&B	C&W
10/57	You Send Me	Keen	*	*	
10/57	Summertime	Keen			
12/57	Desire Me/(I Love You) for Sentimental Reasons	Keen		*	
3/58	Lonely Island/You Were Made for Me	Keen		*	
8/58	Win Your Love for Me	Keen		*	
11/58	Love You Most of All	Keen		*	
3/59	Everybody Likes to Cha-Cha-Cha	Keen		*	
7/59	Only Sixteen	Keen		*	
11/59	There, I've Said It Again	Keen			
5/60	Wonderful World	Keen	*	*	
3/60	Teenage Sonata	RCA			
8/60	Chain Gang	RCA	*	*	
12/60	Sad Mood	RCA			
4/61	That's It, I Quit, I'm Movin' On	RCA			
6/61	Cupid	RCA	*	*	
10/61	Feel It	RCA			
2/62	Twistin' the Night Away	RCA	*	*	
6/62	Bring It on Home to Me	RCA	*	*	
6/62	Having a Party	RCA	*	*	
9/62	Somebody Have Mercy	RCA		*	
9/62	Nothing Can Change This Love	RCA	*	*	

Date	Song	Label	Pop	R&B	C&W
1/63	Send Me Some Lovin'	RCA	°	°	
4/63	Another Saturday Night	RCA	°	°	
7/63	Frankie and Johnny	RCA	°	°	
10/63	Little Red Rooster	RCA	°	°	
1/64	Ain't That Good News?	RCA	°		
6/64	Good Times	RCA	°		
1/65	Shake	RCA	°	°	
1/65	A Change Is Gonna Come	RCA		°	
4/65	It's Got the Whole World Shakin'	RCA		°	
6/65	Sugar Dumpling	RCA		°	

ALBUMS

Date	Album	Label
3/1/58	*Sam Cooke Sings*	Keen
10/20/62	*The Best of Sam Cooke*	RCA Victor
7/24/65	*The Best of Sam Cooke Volume 2*	RCA Victor

The Rock 'n' Roll Years: 1954–1963

4

1954—Changing Times

Rhythm and blues tunes to become popular in 1954 were "Sh-Boom" by the Chords and "Gee" and "I Love You So" by the Crows. These songs were no longer limited to the R&B charts. Their success spread to the upper reaches of the pop charts.

Of course, there were some R&B songs which had been popular with white audiences before 1954. "Money Honey" by the Drifters in 1953 and "One Mint Julep" by the Clovers in 1952 were R&B hits that appeared on some pop charts. During the same period, a young white singer had a two-sided hit that topped both

A 1954 Chevrolet

the pop and R&B surveys. Johnny Ray, who was partially deaf, sold four million copies of "Cry" and "The Little White Cloud That Cried." Ray's performances were emotional pleas which included choking and crying. This raw style appealed greatly to young people. Ray seemed to communicate in a way that was more real than most pop singers. His popularity may have been a sign of things to come. His appeal to black audiences was another sign that racial barriers were beginning to come down in popular music.

By 1954, Bill Haley had several hits in a new style which combined country music with R&B. "Crazy Man Crazy" (1953) may have been the first rock 'n' roll record by a white performer to become popular. In 1954, Haley had an even bigger hit with a cover of Joe Turner's "Shake Rattle and Roll." Haley's version was quite a bit faster than Turner's and his lyrics were a good deal cleaner. Haley was interested in the slang words and the dance beat of the song. He did not, however, want to offend parents or radio pro-

Hank Ballard and the Midnighters were the most popular R&B performers of the year but their records received no pop air play. ("Bleecker" Bob Plotnik Collection)

grammers. He knew that many stations looked for any excuse to avoid playing rock 'n' roll.

"Shake Rattle and Roll" is only one example of an R&B song that was outsold by a white cover record. Like the Midnighters' "Work with Me Annie" and "Annie Had a Baby," Turner's lyrics were considered too suggestive for pop stations. On the other hand, many white cover records simply copied popular R&B songs. The Crew Cuts' copy of "Sh-Boom" outsold the Chords, just as Georgia Gibbs's "Tweedle Dee" outsold LaVern Baker's original record. Both of these covers were almost exact copies of the words and music of the originals. These songs had no suggestive words, but white radio stations seemed to favor white artists whenever possible. In many cases, the covers were so well promoted that listeners never heard the originals. The success of these copy records indicates the shift in many listeners' tastes toward R&B. The fact that there were only several hundred black DJs compared with 10,000 white disc jockeys may explain why so many R&B records were outsold by white copies. In spite of this, more R&B records crossed over to pop in 1954 than in any previous year.

There were changes taking place between blacks and whites in other areas besides music. On May 17, 1954, the Supreme Court of the United States declared segregation in public schools illegal. In their decision, the Court stated that "educational facilities which are separate but equal have no place in public education. Separate educational facilities are inherently unequal." Several months later, the White Citizens' Council began to organize in the South in order to resist the integration of schools. This same organization was involved in banning rock 'n' roll music.

Black and white were not the only colors that Americans were concerned with in the fifties. There was a widespread fear of Red (Communist) attacks and Red spies. Although there was evidence of some Russian spies working in this country, the danger of the situation was greatly exaggerated. The man who was mainly responsible for this Red scare was Senator Joseph McCarthy of Wisconsin. In 1950, McCarthy read a list of 205 names of State Department employees who were members of the Communist Party. During the next four years, panic spread throughout the country. Many books were banned and authors blacklisted. People

LaVern Baker (Billy
Vera Collection)

in all walks of life lost their jobs when seen with somebody with "suspicious" political leanings. Although McCarthy never convicted a single person, his accusations ruined the lives of thousands of men and women. Many of these people never recovered from the damage done to them during this witch-hunt.

The Army–McCarthy Hearings, conducted by the Senate in 1954, served to discredit the senator. A committee was set up to look into the army's charge of blackmail against McCarthy. The hearings were broadcast on national television over a period of several months. The nation watched and listened as army counsel Joseph Welch asked McCarthy: "Have you no sense of decency sir, at long last? Have you left no sense of decency?" McCarthy simply shrugged this off, but all those who watched sensed that this man was finally finished.

The hearings helped to put an end to McCarthy's reign of terror. But the atmosphere he created still existed in this country. A national survey conducted in late 1954 showed that three out of four Americans thought it was a good idea to report friends and relatives to the FBI whom they suspected of being Communists. Expressions like "better dead than Red" were common until the late fifties.

The Army–McCarthy Hearings were not the only big television show of 1954. In December, the first Davy Crockett show was aired on the "Disneyland" television show. Some 40 million Americans watched Fess Parker play the role of the western hero. Many fads came out of the show, including Davy Crockett caps and jackets. The show's theme song, "The Ballad of Davy Crockett," sold over four million copies. Television was now so popular that one frozen food company began marketing the first TV dinner, consisting of turkey, sweet potato, and peas. The meal was heated and served in the same foil plate so that the viewer could keep watching his favorite programs.

Nineteen fifty-four was a good year for movies. There was *On the Waterfront* with Marlon Brando and an all-star cast. There was also *The Caine Mutiny* with Humphrey Bogart and *The Country Girl* with Grace Kelly and Bing Crosby. That year also saw the debut of James Dean in *East of Eden*. Dean became one of the biggest idols of the fifties, although he appeared in only three films. He seemed to represent the misunderstood teenage rebel.

He had a sexy brooding look that was not unlike Elvis's. But Dean did not live long enough to reach his potential as a superstar. In 1955, he died in a car crash, the victim of his own reckless driving. After his death, he seemed to become even more of an idol.

The top songs of 1954 were still mostly traditional ballads. These included "Little Things Mean a Lot," Kitty Kallen; "Hey There," Rosemary Cloony; "Wanted," Perry Como; and "Secret Love," Doris Day. The Crew Cuts' version of "Sh-Boom" made the top ten, while Bill Haley's "Shake Rattle and Roll" was among the twenty-five most popular records of the year.

All in all, 1954 was a turning point in many ways. The groundwork had been laid for political and social changes. Movie idols looked and acted tougher and more rebellious. Although people were turning from radio to TV for entertainment and information, radio had become the hub of the new teenage culture. Rock 'n' roll had come to stay.

MAJOR EVENTS OF 1954

Politics and Government

Army–McCarthy Hearings broadcast on national television. Twenty million Americans watch as McCarthy is discredited by the U.S. Senate.

Brown v. *Board of Education of Topeka.* The Supreme Court rules that separate educational facilities on the basis of race are unequal and illegal.

The Senate defeats a constitutional amendment to give eighteen-year-olds the right to vote. Young people ask, "If we are old enough to fight and die for our country, why can't we vote?"

President Eisenhower announces that the first hydrogen bomb was dropped in the Pacific some two years earlier. Shortly thereafter, a similar bomb is tested in the Marshall Islands.

Democrats gain a majority in both houses of Congress.

In the News

Three Puerto Rican nationalists fire from the visitors' gallery in the House of Representatives and injure five congressmen.

The words "under God" are added to the Pledge of Allegiance. Some scientists believe that cigarette smoking is linked to lung cancer.

The Arts

Academy Award for best film goes to *On the Waterfront.* Marlon Brando wins best-actor award for the same film. Grace Kelly is the best actress for her role in *The Country Girl.* Other memorable movies are *The Caine Mutiny,* with Humphrey Bogart; *Rebel Without a Cause,* with James Dean; and *The Wild One,* with Marlon Brando.

Ernest Hemingway wins the Nobel Prize for Literature.

Television

Almost 30 million people now own television sets. In 1946 there had been fewer than 7,000 sets in American homes.

A meeting of the President's Cabinet is shown on television for the first time.

The first episode of Davy Crockett is aired on Walt Disney's "Disneyland" show.

The first live telecast of the Miss America Contest, hosted by Bert Parks, is aired from Atlantic City, New Jersey.

Some of the most popular television shows of this year are situation comedies: "Father Knows Best" starring Robert Young, "December Bride," with Spring Byington, and "Private Secretary" with Ann Southern.

Sports

Rocky Marciano retains his heavyweight boxing crown.

The New York Yankees lose the pennant to the Cleveland Indians after winning the last five American League flags.

A new magazine, *Sports Illustrated,* makes its debut.

The Cleveland Browns defeat the Detroit Lions 56 to 10 to win the NFL championship.

Fads and Fashions

In an attempt to smell good, people consume large quantities of chlorophyll. Claims are made that this "miracle" substance makes people odorless. Chlorophyll is added to soaps, mouthwash, and chewing gum.

Psychoanalysis is extremely popular in 1954. Words like ego, inferiority complex, and shrink become part of everyday conversation.

Pedal pushers are the rage in women's clothing. Members of both sexes begin showing off their legs with Bermuda shorts—abbreviated, baggy pants cut above the knees and often worn with knee-high nylon socks.

TOP ROCK 'N' ROLL RECORDS OF 1954

Song	Artist	Record Label
Annie Had a Baby	The Midnighters	Federal
Dim Dim the Lights	Bill Haley and the Comets	Decca
Earth Angel	The Penguins	Dootone
Gee	The Crows	Rama
Gloria	The Cadillacs	Josie
Goodnight Sweetheart Goodnight	The Spaniels	Vee Jay
Honey Love	The Drifters	Atlantic
Lovey Dovey	The Clovers	Atlantic
Pledging My Love	Johnny Ace	Duke
Sexy Ways	The Midnighters	Federal
Shake Rattle and Roll	Joe Turner	Atlantic
Sh-Boom	The Chords	Cat
Sincerely	The Moonglows	Chess
Things That I Used to Do	Eddie "Guitar Slim" Jones	Specialty
Tweedle Dee	LaVern Baker	Atlantic
Work with Me Annie	The Midnighters	Federal
Life Is But a Dream	The Harptones	Paradise
Your Cash Ain't Nothin' But Trash	The Clovers	Atlantic

5

1955—Rock Around the Clock

Rock 'n' roll took a giant step forward in 1955. There were more pop hit records in authentic R&B styles than ever before. A good number of the more successful songs were covered by pop performers. In some cases, the copy-cats outsold the original artist. Gale Storm, TV's "My Little Margie," outsold Smiley Lewis's "I Hear You Knockin'." Meanwhile, Pat Boone's "Ain't That a Shame" was more popular than Fats Domino's original version. But at the same time, a growing number of rock 'n' roll fans were buying the original records.

Two records that were released in late 1954 became giant hits during the following year: "Earth Angel" and "Pledging My Love." The Penguins' recording of Jesse Belvin's "Earth Angel" is one of the most memorable vocal group songs. In a 1977 poll taken by radio station WCBS-FM of the 500 most popular songs of all time, "Earth Angel" was number two. The version that the listeners remembered was by the Penguins. The Crew Cuts' version of the song could not match the original in either sales or soul.

"Pledging My Love" by Johnny Ace followed the Penguins' record to the top of the charts. Ace was a black ballad singer who gained a huge R&B audience in the early fifties. He had a cool but plaintive vocal style. Ace sang "Pledging My Love" with both tenderness and pain. The Johnny Otis orchestra played tastefully

Dancers demonstrate the popular Lindy to the rockin' sounds of Bill Haley and the Comets. (Courtesy of Columbia Pictures)

in the background. "Pledging My Love" became one of the most popular songs of 1955.

As the months passed, a good number of rock 'n' roll songs made their way to the top of the pop charts. Chuck Berry had his first hit, "Maybellene." The Nutmegs, from New Haven, Connecticut, had their first and only hit with "Story Untold." The Platters' "Only You" was to be one of many number one singles for the group. There was also LaVern Baker with "Bop Ting-a-Ling," Etta James with "Wallflower," and Nappy Brown's "Don't Be Angry." There were also some novelty songs with a rock 'n' roll beat that were successful in 1955. These included "Ling Ting Tong," the Five Keys, and "At My Front Door," the El Dorados.

As more and more R&B artists began to have pop hits, the music business changed its attitude toward rock 'n' roll. Before 1955, these artists would have needed to look at the back of the music-trade magazines (*Cashbox* and *Billboard*) to find their songs. This was where the R&B charts were placed. But now, a growing number of black performers could find their hit records listed on the pop charts in the front of these magazines. At the same time, black people in the South began to move from the back of segregated buses into the front. This movement soon extended into all areas of American life.

Late in 1955, a black woman boarded a public bus in Montgomery, Alabama. Instead of moving to the back of the bus, where blacks were required to sit, she took a seat up front. When she refused to give up her seat to a white man, she was arrested. The minister of a local church called a meeting of black residents in order to discuss the incident. This minister was Martin Luther King, Jr., and the result of the meeting was a boycott of all Montgomery buses by black people.

For over one year, the black people of Montgomery refused to ride on public buses. This caused great hardships to the black community and large financial losses to the city of Montgomery. King was fined and convicted of conducting an illegal boycott. He was the target of many threats; at one point, his house was bombed. Yet he continued to urge his followers to demonstrate peacefully. In one of his most moving speeches, he declared:

> If we are arrested every day, if we are exploited every day, if we are trampled over every day, don't ever let anyone pull you so low as to hate them. We must use the moral weapon of love. We must have compassion and understanding for those who hate us. We must realize that so many people are taught to hate us that they are not totally responsible for their hate. But we stand in life at midnight. We are always at the threshold of a new dawn.

After waiting for over a year, King and his followers tasted victory. The Supreme Court ruled that Alabama's bus segregation laws were unconstitutional. Rosa Parks, who started the whole thing, was photographed sitting in the front of a Montgomery bus. Other cities in the South soon desegregated their buses. More important, a big step was taken in the civil rights cause. Dr. King and his followers had proved that progress could be made without taking violent action. But these people understood that change never comes easily.

Integration was taking place on the music scene too. Just as white listeners were buying rhythm and blues records, black listeners were responding to white rock 'n' roll. The biggest hit of the year was "Rock Around the Clock" by Bill Haley and the Comets. The song topped the pop, R&B, and country charts in 1955. "Rock Around the Clock" was the top record of the year and one of the most popular of all time. It seemed to capture the mood and excitement of young people. Because it was the theme song of the movie, *Blackboard Jungle,* many adults linked it with teenage crime. Nobody has ever really shown a link between rock 'n' roll and juvenile delinquency. For many adults, the music was loud and rowdy. But to young people, rock 'n' roll was new and exciting.

In 1955, there were fewer conventional ballad hits than in most other years. The most popular ballad of the year was "Unchained Melody" by Roy Hamilton. The song did not have a strong beat, but was closer in feeling to a slow R&B song than to a conventional ballad. Novelty songs were big in 1955: Tennessee Ernie Ford did a lively version of "Sixteen Tons," which was a big hit; Bill Hayes's "Ballad of Davy Crockett" was an even bigger hit. Bandleader Prez Prado struck gold with a cha-cha, "Cherry Pink

The Moonglows had several popular records in 1955, including "Most of All." ("Bleecker" Bob Plotnik Collection)

and Apple Blossom White." Bearded Mitch Miller did the same with "The Yellow Rose of Texas." Two of the year's more popular ballads were "A Blossom Fell," Nat King Cole, and an instrumental version of "Autumn Leaves" by the pianist Roger Williams.

As 1955 came to a close, rock 'n' roll seemed to be coming into its own. The older generation still believed it was just a passing fad. Most of the established record companies felt the same way. They were sure that this crazy noise would quiet down and people would return to listening to "good" music. But it was too late to turn the tide. Rock 'n' roll had taken over, as teenagers all over the world were rocking around the clock.

MAJOR EVENTS OF 1955

Politics and Government

The U.S. begins sending financial aid to South Vietnam, amounting to $216 million.

A summit conference between the major world powers is held in Geneva. It is attended by the heads of state of France, Great Britain, the U.S., and the U.S.S.R. Tensions in the cold war between Russia and the Western powers ease for the moment.

Rosa Parks refuses to give up her seat to a white man on a Montgomery, Alabama, bus. The black community, led by the Reverend Martin Luther King, Jr., stages a 54-week boycott of public buses in Montgomery.

In the News

Dr. Jonas Salk develops an effective polio vaccine.

The AFL and CIO combine. George Meany heads up these merged labor unions.

A fourteen-year-old black youth is kidnapped from his Mississippi home for having "whistled at a white woman." Several days later, his body is found in the Tallahatchie River. The two white men accused of the murder are acquitted by an all-white jury.

President Eisenhower suffers a heart attack while vacationing in Denver.

The Arts

Academy Award for best film goes to *Marty*. Ernest Borgnine is best actor in the title role. Anna Magnani wins best-actress award for her performance in *The Rose Tattoo*. James Dean, nominated for an Oscar for his performance in *East of Eden*, dies in a car crash.

Marian Anderson becomes the first black singer to perform at the Metropolitan Opera in New York.

Charlie Parker, the most innovative jazz saxophone player of his era, dies at thirty-four.

Television

President Eisenhower conducts the first televised news conference.

NBC-TV broadcasts "Peter Pan" in "compatible color." The show stars Mary Martin in the title role.

"Gunsmoke" makes its television debut. This western series stars James Arness and Amanda Blake. Other top-rated westerns this year are "The Rifleman" and "Wyatt Earp."

Some important new shows to appear in 1955 were "You'll Never Get Rich," starring Phil Silvers as the fast-talking Sergeant Bilko; "Alfred Hitchcock Presents"; "The Mickey Mouse Club"; "Mike Wallace Interviews"; "The Lawrence Welk Show"; "Captain Kangaroo"; and "Lassie."

Sports

The Brooklyn Dodgers beat the New York Yankees to capture their first World Series.

Don Larson of the Yankees pitches the first perfect game in a World Series.

The Cleveland Browns defeat the Los Angeles Rams and win the NFL title for the second straight year.

Fads and Fashions

The color pink is the big news in men's fashions. There are pink shirts, pink ties, and even charcoal gray suits with specks of pink.

Marilyn Monroe is firmly established as the most important sex symbol of the era.

Horror comics are extremely popular among the young. Parental objections to this gory entertainment will end this fad in the next few years.

TOP ROCK 'N' ROLL RECORDS OF 1955

Song	Artist	Record Label
Ain't That a Shame	Fats Domino	Imperial
At My Front Door	El Dorados	Vee Jay
Bo Diddley	Bo Diddley	Chess
Bop Ting-a-Ling	LaVern Baker	Atlantic
Devil or Angel	The Clovers	Atlantic
Don't Be Angry	Nappy Brown	Savoy
Flip Flop and Fly	Joe Turner	Atlantic
Hearts of Stone	The Charms	DeLuxe
I Hear You Knockin'	Smiley Lewis	Imperial
Ko Ko Mo	Gene and Eunice	Aladdin
Ling Ting Tong	The Charms	Deluxe
Maybellene	Chuck Berry	Chess
Most of All	The Moonglows	Chess
Only You	The Platters	Mercury
Rock Around the Clock	Bill Haley and the Comets	Decca
Speedo	The Cadillacs	Josie
The Great Pretender	The Platters	Mercury
Tutti Frutti	Little Richard	Specialty
Unchained Melody	Roy Hamilton	Epic
Wallflower	Etta James	Modern

1956—The Big Beat

Rock 'n' roll had come to stay in 1956. More than half of the year's top hits were songs with "the big beat." In January, the most popular songs in the country were Tennessee Ernie Ford's "Sixteen Tons" and Dean Martin's "Memories Are Made of This." Tennessee Ernie's record featured his low, good-natured voice and a snappy beat. "Sixteen Tons" was not, however, a rock 'n' roll song. The Platters' "Great Pretender" was very popular early in 1956, but bandleader Nelson Riddle had an even bigger hit at the same time—"Lisbon Antigua" was a cute instrumental novelty. Les Baxter's "The Poor People of Paris" was the same kind of tune. Together, these two songs dominated the charts during March and April. They were soon replaced by "Blue Suede Shoes" and "Heartbreak Hotel."

These new songs seemed to explode over the airwaves. In "Blue Suede Shoes," Carl Perkins seemed to be speaking in a language that only the young could understand. The song was really about a guy who was demanding the right to express his own style. That is what teenagers seemed to be looking for—the right to have their own tastes. The words to the song might just as well have said: "Don't break my new rock 'n' roll records."

Nobody expressed the new style better than Elvis Presley. He was tough-looking and his music was tough-sounding. Elvis was idolized by teenage boys and adored by the girls. Considering Presley's incredible popularity, it is not surprising that his version of "Blue Suede Shoes" outsold Carl Perkins's. "Heartbreak Hotel," which was released one month before Elvis covered "Blue Suede Shoes," was an even bigger hit. The only record in 1956 which was bigger than "Heartbreak Hotel" was another Presley song, "Don't Be Cruel."

When record companies saw Elvis's amazing sales figures, they were forced to recognize a change in the record-buying public. Teenagers were simply not going to buy the same music as their parents. The record companies, therefore, had to respond to the tastes of the young audience. Capitol came up with "Be-Bop-a-Lula" by Gene Vincent. The singer and the song sounded so much like Elvis, many people thought that it was. Meanwhile, Elvis was moving ahead. He made his first movie, *Love Me Tender,* and recorded the title song. The melody was taken from an old folk song called "Aura Lee." It soon became Elvis's first ballad hit. "Love Me Tender" revealed a softer side of Elvis and hinted that he was also interested in appealing to the tastes of the older generation. But for the most part, adults disliked Elvis. They could not trust anybody who could shake his hips and sing this "crazy rock 'n' roll stuff."

The fact that Elvis was a white man singing rock 'n' roll seemed to make all the difference. He was too big to be hurt by radio station bans. However, many black artists were still not being played by radio stations that were against rock 'n' roll. Little Richard,

The new teenage lifestyle of the fifties as depicted by the cast of *Grease*
(Courtesy of *Grease*, Broadway's longest running musical)

with his raw sound and his wild performances, found his music banned by many stations. The fact that his records were making the charts proves that listeners really wanted to hear authentic rock 'n' roll. In 1955, Pat Boone's cover of "Tutti Frutti" had outsold Little Richard's original. But in 1956, Boone's bland copy of "Long Tall Sally" was less popular than Richard's authentic version. The kids wanted to hear the *real* big beat. They got what they wanted.

There were popular rock 'n' roll records of all kinds in 1956. There was the New Orleans sound of Clarence "Frogman" Henry, "Ain't Got No Home," and Shirley and Lee's "Let the Good Times Roll." There were a good many doo-wop hits as well. Both the Platters and Frankie Lymon and the Teenagers had several big hits that year. There were also the Teen Queens' "Eddie My Love"; the Cleftones' "Little Girl of Mine"; the Turbans' "When You Dance"; and the Willows' "Church Bells May Ring." This is just a partial list of doo-wop groups that had big hits in 1956. The most important slow vocal group record of the year was the Five Satins' "In the Still of the Night." The song had a rich harmony sound and an emotional performance by lead singer Fred Paris. Many rock critics rate "In the Still of the Night" the greatest slow doo-wop song of the mid-fifties. But the listeners of WCBS-FM selected the song as their number one *all-time* favorite.

Aside from the giant explosion in popular music, 1956 was a pretty quiet year. Relations between the U.S. and the U.S.S.R. seemed to be easing. Russian Premier Nikita Khrushchev made a goodwill tour of the West and opened his nation to foreign tourists

A typical American living room circa 1956, featuring that all-important TV set

and reporters. The Montgomery bus boycott was still in progress, but many northerners were hopeful that integration was around the corner. Most Americans felt that Ike would have no trouble winning a second term as president, if his health improved. The economy was slowing down after a few boom years. But in the record business, sales had never been better.

Several Hollywood stars were making the headlines in 1956. Actress Grace Kelly married Prince Ranier and became Princess Grace of Monaco. Sex goddess Marilyn Monroe married playwright Arthur Miller, after recently divorcing baseball's "Jolting Joe" DiMaggio. But Elvis was making even bigger news. He had become the most talked-about personality in America. Together with his manager, Colonel Tom Parker, Elvis marketed hats, T-shirts, book-ends, and pictures that glowed in the dark. He was the king of "the big beat."

MAJOR EVENTS OF 1956

Politics and Government

Ike is reelected to a second term as President. For the second time in a row, he defeats Democratic candidate Adlai Stevenson. Eisenhower is so popular that even Stevenson admits that he likes Ike.

"Freedom fighters" revolt against Soviet rule in Hungary. After several short-lived victories by the rebels, Russian tanks move in and crush the uprising.

War breaks out in the Middle East. Israel, France, and Great Britain invade Egypt in an attempt to regain possession of the Suez Canal. America pressures the three countries to withdraw their troops.

Soviet leader Khrushchev denounces former Premier Stalin and opens Russia to foreign reporters, merchants, and tourists.

In the News

Dr. Albert Sabin discovers an oral polio vaccine.

Fifty lives are lost when the Italian ship *Andrea Doria* collides with the Swedish liner *Stockholm*.

The University of Alabama expels its first black student, Autherine Lucy, after several campus disturbances over the admission of blacks.

The Arts

A new group of American-bred bohemians emerges and calls itself "the beat generation" or "beatniks." Their leaders include writers Jack Kerouac and Allen Ginsberg.

Around the World in Eighty Days wins the Academy Award for best picture. Yul Brynner is the best actor for his performance in *The King and I.* Ingrid Bergman wins best-actress award for her role in *Anastasia.* Other popular films include *The Ten Commandments, Bus Stop,* and *The Seventh Seal.*

The year's most popular books are *Peyton Place* by Grace Metalious, *Must You Conform?* by Robert Lindner, and *Don't Go Near the Water* by William Brinkley.

Works of innovative artists, especially that of Jackson Pollack, move the capital of the art world from Paris to New York.

Television

Nineteen fifty-six marks television's tenth year. Some 20,000 Americans buy TV sets daily. Statistics show that many people spend more time watching TV than working.

One of the most important dramatic TV series has its debut in 1956. "Playhouse 90's" first production is a play called *Forbidden Games,* written by Rod Serling and starring Charlton Heston. The second "Playhouse 90" production is an even bigger blockbuster: *Requiem for a Heavyweight,* also written by Serling, stars Jack Palance, Kim Stanley, and Ed Wynn. The show wins many TV awards and is later made into a successful movie.

Quiz shows are extremely popular, especially "21" and the "$64,000 Question." Game shows like "Truth or Consequences" and "The Price Is Right" also attract many viewers.

Sports

The 1956 Olympic summer games are held in Melbourne, Australia. War in the Middle East and uprisings in Hungary reduce the number of participating countries from 75 to 67.

Floyd Patterson wins the heavyweight boxing crown vacated by undefeated Rocky Marciano.

The New York Yankees beat the Brooklyn Dodgers in seven games to capture the 1956 World Series crown.

New York Giants defeat Chicago Bears 47 to 7 and capture the NFL championship.

Fads and Fashions

The late James Dean becomes a fad hero. A book called *James Dean Returns* sells over 50,000 copies. People pay a quarter to see the car he died in and another quarter to sit behind its wheel.

Adults go crazy over trading stamps. Every time they go food shopping, they receive stamps. These are then pasted in booklets and exchanged for merchandise.

Going steady is a big fad among teens. In order to show their deep attachments, young people exchange I.D. bracelets, ankle chains, and class rings.

Longer and pointier shoes are the rage in women's fashions. Some ladies are sporting spiked heels of three inches and more.

TOP ROCK 'N' ROLL RECORDS OF 1956

Song	Artist	Record Label
A Casual Look	The Sixteens	Flip
Ain't Got No Home	Clarence "Frogman" Henry	Argo
Be-Bop-a-Lula	Gene Vincent	Capitol
Blue Suede Shoes	Carl Perkins	Sun
Church Bells May Ring	The Willows	Melba
Don't Be Cruel	Elvis Presley	RCA
Eddie My Love	The Teen Queens	RMP
Fever	Little Willie John	King
Heartbreak Hotel	Elvis Presley	RCA
Honky Tonk	Bill Doggett	King
Hound Dog	Elvis Presley	RCA
I'm in Love Again	Fats Domino	Imperial
In the Still of the Night	The Five Satins	Ember
Let the Good Times Roll	Shirley and Lee	Aladdin
Little Girl of Mine	The Cleftones	Gee

Song	Artist	Record Label
Long Tall Sally	Little Richard	Specialty
Stranded in the Jungle	The Cadets	Modern
The Closer You Are	The Channels	Whirlin' Disc
Treasure of Love	Clyde McPhatter	Atlantic
When You Dance	Turbans	Herald
Why Do Fools Fall in Love	Frankie Lymon and the Teenagers	Gee
Since I Met You Baby	Ivory Joe Hunter	Atlantic

7

1957—The Beat Goes On

Rock 'n' roll continued to grow in 1957. Bright new stars like Sam Cooke, Jerry Lee Lewis, and the Everly Brothers established themselves as hit makers. More vocal groups were doing well on the charts. The Del Vikings had two big hits with "Come Go with Me" and "Whispering Bells." The Coasters introduced their unique sound with a two-sided smash, "Searchin'" and "Young Blood." They became one of the few black vocal groups to have hits over a period of several years. A vocal duo, Mickey and Sylvia, had a big hit in 1957 with "Love Is Strange." The song had a Latin beat which many adults called the cha-cha. The younger listeners and dancers preferred the name calypso. This type of a beat was used on many hit records in 1957. These included "Diana," Paul Anka; "Marianne," Terry Gilkyson; and "The Banana Boat Song," Harry Belafonte.

In 1957, many record companies tried to present clean-cut-looking rock 'n' roll singers with clean-cut sounds. The best of these new rockers were the Everly Brothers. They had an authentic vocal sound and skillful record producers. They had duck-tail haircuts like Elvis, but their sound was innocent, not tough. Ricky Nelson, who looked even more like Elvis, began a successful recording career with a cover of Fats Domino's "I'm Walkin'." Like the Everlys, Nelson developed a sound that owed a great deal to country music.

There were several hits with a C&W flavor in 1957. One of the

Mickey and Sylvia ("Bleecker" Bob Plotnik Collection)

most popular was "Young Love," Sonny James. The song had teenage lyrics, but was more country than rock 'n' roll. On the other hand, Buddy Knox's "Party Doll" and Jimmy Bowen's "I'm Sticking with You" had a definite rock beat. These songs marked the beginning of the Tex-Mex sound. Later in the year, that sound was expanded by Buddy Holly and the Crickets.

Buddy Holly has become one of the most admired rock 'n' roll performers of all time. From the beginning, Holly was influenced by Elvis, but there were important differences. Holly's vocal sound was intense but not tough. His skinny kid with glasses image was in sharp contrast to Elvis's sex appeal. His three hits in 1957—"That'll Be the Day," "Peggy Sue," and "Oh Boy"—also did well on the R&B charts. Holly proved that you did not have to be black, tough, or good-looking to be an authentic rock 'n' roll star. Sometimes, talent was enough.

Established rock 'n' roll performers had a good year in 1957. Elvis's "All Shook Up" was the top song of the year on most charts, and three other Presley tunes made the top twenty—"Too Much," "Teddy Bear," and "Jailhouse Rock." Fats Domino also had three hits that year—"I'm Walkin'," "Blueberry Hill," and "Blue Monday." Chuck Berry's "School Days" also did well in 1957. Meanwhile, Pat Boone, the original clean-cut rocker, had two top hits—"Love Letters in the Sand" and "Don't Forbid Me." Both songs were traditional ballads. Boone no longer needed to cover R&B tunes.

The most interesting cover record of 1957 was "Little Darlin' " by the Diamonds. The Canadian group's record was an exact duplication of the Gladiolas' original. Lead singer Maurice Williams's unique high voice highlighted this Latin-tinged novelty, but the Diamonds' record greatly outsold the original to become one of the year's biggest hits. Soulful Sam Cooke switched from gospel to rock 'n' roll in 1957. His smooth style made "You Send

The Gladiolas ("Bleecker" Bob Plotnik Collection)

Me" one of the top twenty records of the year. Jerry Lee Lewis also made the charts with his first release, "Whole Lotta Shakin' Goin' On."

Many adults definitely felt that there was too much "shakin' " going on in rock 'n' roll. They preferred traditional popular music. Perry Como had a popular TV show and also a top record in 1957, "Round and Round." Jimmy Dorsey, a popular big bandleader in the forties, had an instrumental hit, "So Rare." A couple of new singers had hits that seemed to appeal to both adults and teen-agers. Jimmie Rodgers had a sweet, pure voice. The music on records like "Honeycomb" and "Kisses Sweeter Than Wine" had a lively folk quality. But this definitely was not rock 'n' roll. Johnny Mathis's records were usually slow and dreamy. Though Mathis was similar to other ballad singers, he seemed to project a roman-tic feeling to young people. His singles—"Chances Are," "Won-derful Wonderful," and "It's Not for Me to Say"—were big hits in 1957. His first album—*Johnny's Greatest Hits*—was a best seller for several years. There seemed to be room on the charts for differ-ent kinds of music by a variety of performers. The music business was having another good year.

Economic conditions in 1957 were not so good in many other areas of American life. The nation had just gone through a period of enormous spending. Everyone seemed to be cutting back. The automobile industry was trying to build economical cars instead of fast ones. Prices were up, but wages were only $82.50 a week for the average factory worker. Most people were feeling the squeeze in their pocketbooks.

There were other problems aside from finances in 1957. The So-viet Union announced the successful launching of Sputnik, the first manmade satellite, into space. The U.S. feared that it was los-ing the space race, and there was much talk about a "science gap." One month later, the Soviets launched Sputnik II, an even heavier satellite. This time there was a passenger on board, a dog named Laika. The Soviet Union seemed only one step away from sending a man into space. Although the U.S. congratulated the U.S.S.R. for these accomplishments, there was a growing fear that the prestige of America was declining.

Americans traditionally believed that they were the number one nation in the world. But the Russians were demonstrating that

Johnny Mathis—the king of "make out" music (Courtesy of *Record World* magazine)

this might not be true. Americans responded by trying to improve education. Science and math courses became more important. Algebra and geometry were taught in the early grades. Some schools even changed their hours, adding extra classes and cutting out free periods. The attitude seemed to be that this country was too permissive with its young people. Russian schools were pictured as being much tougher and stricter with their students. In 1957, America was trying to close the gap in the education race. But there were still other problems in American schools.

When the Supreme Court ordered the integration of public schools in 1954, they demanded that local governments comply "with all deliberate speed." Three years later, the schools of Little Rock, Arkansas, were just beginning to desegregate. The first step was to be the admission of nine black students to the all-white Central High. The resistance to integration in the South was so great President Eisenhower sent 1,000 paratroopers to Little Rock in the hope of preventing violence. Two dozen paratroopers remained in Central High for the entire school year.

The integration of Little Rock was the last major civil rights event of the fifties. Many young white people seemed to identify with the civil rights movement. In the South, students adjusted to integration better than their parents. Perhaps young people could better understand the search for equal rights.

MAJOR EVENTS OF 1957

Politics and Government

President Eisenhower sends 1,000 Army paratroopers to Little Rock, Arkansas, to protect the first black students attending an all-white high school.

Fidel Castro leads a revolt against Cuban dictator Juan Batista.

Ike issues Eisenhower Doctrine to prevent the spread of Communism in the Middle East.

Congress passes the first new civil rights bill in 82 years. The new legislation calls for the establishment of a civil rights commission.

In the News

Russians send Sputnik I—the first space satellite—into orbit, and the space race begins.

As the first American nuclear test takes place in Nevada, a group of scientists launches an international protest to "ban the bomb." The group hopes to put a stop to all nuclear testing around the world.

A major earthquake shakes the city of San Francisco.

George Metesky—New York's "mad bomber"—is caught after 16 years and 32 bombings.

An economic recession begins and extends into late 1958.

The Arts

The Academy Award for the year's best movie goes to *The Bridge on the River Kwai*. Alec Guinness is the year's best actor for his role in the film. Joanne Woodward wins the best-actress award for her performance in *The Three Faces of Eve*. Other notable movies are *Twelve Angry Men, And God Created Woman*, starring French sex symbol Brigitte Bardot, and *The Incredible Shrinking Man*.

Senator John F. Kennedy wins a Pulitzer Prize for his book, *Profiles in Courage*. The best-selling book of the year is James Gould Cozzens' *By Love Possessed*. Art Linkletter's *Kids Say the Darnedest Things* outsells all other nonfiction books.

One of the top Broadway musicals of the year is *The Music Man*. The play tells the story of a square con-man, who is a musician in a small American town.

Television

Courtroom drama comes to TV with Erle Stanley Gardner's "Perry Mason." The series stars Raymond Burr as the clever and dedicated lawyer. Although the show runs for many years, Mason appears never to lose a case.

A real courtroom drama unfolds on TV as Robert Kennedy interrogates underworld figures and union leaders during the investigations of the Senate Rackets Committee.

Westerns are bigger than ever. Some of the new cowboy shows which become popular are "Have Gun, Will Travel" and "Maverick." These shows are geared more for adults than kids. "Maverick," starring James Garner as a cowardly gambler, becomes a great favorite of many older viewers.

A number of situation comedies are quite popular this year. These include "The Real McCoys" and "Leave It to Beaver."

Sports

Jackie Robinson, the first black player in major league baseball, retires after the 1956 season.

The Brooklyn Dodgers move to Los Angeles, and the New York Giants leave the Bronx for San Francisco.

Floyd Patterson retains his heavyweight title as he knocks out opponent Pete Rademacher in the sixth round.

The Milwaukee Braves beat the Yankees in seven games and bring home the World Series crown.

The Detroit Lions defeat the Cleveland Browns 59 to 14 and win the NFL championship.

Fads and Fashion

Americans go contest crazy in 1957. There are eating contests, drinking contests, and staying-awake-the-longest contests.

Another popular fad with the college crowd is panty raids. Boys try to sneak into girls' dorms in order to steal panties, bras, etc. These raids feature a great deal of screaming, and often get the boys suspended from school.

A number of radical hairstyles are popular with both boys and girls. Many guys are sporting flat-top crew cuts, apache-style haircuts, and duck-tails. Girls are also sporting the "Elvis look," in addition to pony tails and "poodle cuts."

The hot look in women's fashion is the sack dress, also known as the chemise. The dress fits loosely, kind of like a bag. Another popular fashion with young girls is plaid pleated mid-calf skirts with matching pullovers and cardigans.

Boys also are fashion conscious. They go to their sock hops and proms (often held in the school gym) in white sport coats and tight, pegged pants.

TOP ROCK 'N' ROLL RECORDS OF 1957

Song	Artist	Record Label
Bony Maronie	Larry Williams	Specialty
Bye Bye Love	Everly Brothers	Cadence
Come Go with Me	The Del Vikings	Dot
Happy, Happy Birthday Baby	The Tune Weavers	Checkers
I'm Stickin' with You	Jimmy Bowen	Roulette
I'm Walkin'	Fats Domino	Imperial
Jailhouse Rock	Elvis Presley	RCA
Jenny Jenny	Little Richard	Specialty
Jim Dandy	LaVern Baker	Atlantic
Just Because	Lloyd Price	ABC Paramount
Keep A-Knockin'	Little Richard	Specialty
Little Bitty Pretty One	Thurston Harris	Aladdin
Little Darlin'	The Gladiolas	Excello
Long Lonely Nights	Lee Andrews and the Hearts	Chess
Love Is Strange	Mickey and Sylvia	Groove
Mr. Lee	The Bobbettes	Atlantic
Party Doll	Buddy Knox	Roulette
Peanuts	Little Joe and the Thrillers	Okeh
Peggy Sue	Buddy Holly	Decca
Raunchy	Bill Justice	Phillips
Rock and Roll Music	Chuck Berry	Chess
School Days	Chuck Berry	Chess
Searchin'	The Coasters	Atlantic
Short Fat Fanny	Larry Williams	Specialty
Susie Q	Dale Hawkins	Checker
That'll Be the Day	Buddy Holly and the Crickets	Brunswick
To the Aisle	The Five Satins	Ember
Wake Up Little Susie	Everly Brothers	Cadence
Whispering Bells	The Del Vikings	Dot
White Sport Coat and a Pink Carnation	Mary Robbins	Columbia
Whole Lotta Shakin' Goin' On	Jerry Lee Lewis	Sun
Young Blood	The Coasters	Atlantic
You Send Me	Sam Cooke	Keen
Desirie	Charts	Everlast

1958—Rockin' on "Bandstand"

Nineteen fifty-eight was a big year for unusual records and new fads. Four of the year's top ten recordings were novelty numbers. A bouncy Italian song, "Volare," by Domenico Modugno, was the biggest hit of the year. Not far behind on the charts was David Seville's tale of his friend, the "Witch Doctor," and Sheb Wolley's "Purple People Eater." Two instrumentals also found their way to the top ten of the year: "Patricia," Perez Prado, and "Tequila," the Champs. Both songs had a Latin beat. "Patricia" was a cha-cha which featured a big orchestra, while "Tequila" was a mambo with a growling sax. At the end of each chorus, the music would stop and a low voice would exclaim, "Tequila." Many of the hits by vocal groups in 1957 were also novelty songs. The Coasters' "Yakety Yak" was both funny and topical, as was the Silhouettes' "Get a Job." The Olympics complained that they could not get a date because all the girls were watching those "Western Movies" on TV. In fact, there were twenty-one westerns on the tube that year.

The sounds coming from the radio seemed to be a little softer in 1958. Perry Como had a two-sided smash, "Catch a Falling Star" and "Magic Moments." Dean Martin, another popular crooner, had a top song with "Return to Me," which was sung partly in Italian. Parents were happy when the Platters recorded two old

A teenage girl sporting her stylish pony tail shows off some of the latest dance steps at her thirteenth birthday party.

standards, "Twilight Time" and "Smoke Gets in Your Eyes." Critics of rock 'n' roll were once again predicting that the music was becoming less popular, but they were wrong. Nineteen fifty-eight turned out to be another big year for teenagers and their music.

The tastes and styles of young people could be seen on television every afternoon. By 1958, "American Bandstand" had become the number one daytime TV program in the country. The show allowed teenagers to follow the activities of people their own age. There were regulars who appeared on the show every day. Viewers came to know who was going steady with whom. Boys would argue about whether Justine or Fran was prettier, while most of the girls preferred Bobby. When one of the "Bandstand" regulars changed hairstyles or clothes, millions of teenagers took note.

Dick Clark always had a guest performer on who would mouth the lyrics to his hit while the record played. This was important to singers of limited ability, since many of them depended on recording-studio tricks. Every important rock 'n' roll artist except Elvis and Ricky Nelson made at least one appearance on "Bandstand." Clark also interviewed his guest stars. This gave fans a chance to hear their favorite performers talk about themselves.

At some point in every show, Clark would select three teenagers to rate records. Three records were played, and the young panel gave them a score from 3.5 to 9.5. Based on his feelings about how popular a record was with his viewers, Clark created his own "American Bandstand Teenage Top 10."

It is not difficult to understand why Dick Clark was the most powerful person in the music business during the late fifties. He had close contact with young people, which helped him to understand their tastes. He also had the power to promote or ignore a record. If a song or dance craze was given good exposure on "Bandstand," it had a good chance of becoming popular. In 1958, the stroll became a popular line-dance on "Bandstand." A short time later, the Diamonds' version of "The Stroll" was a big hit. Kids were buying the record and doing the dance. During the next few years, "Bandstand" would launch a number of popular dance crazes—the Twist, the Fly, the Popeye, and others. In 1958, "Bandstand" popularized the American teenager.

Many new teenage stars became popular. Danny and the Juniors had two big hits with "At the Hop" and "Rock and Roll is Here to Stay." Both songs were geared strictly for teenagers, and both received good exposure on "Bandstand." Another group of teenagers, Dion and the Belmonts, had a hit with "I Wonder Why." The group was from the street corners of the Bronx, and their first release launched the new Laurie record label. A West Coast group, the Teddy Bears, had a hit with "To Know Him Is to Love Him." The song was written by an eighteen-year-old named Phil Spector. Within a short time, Spector would leave the group and go on to become one of the most successful producers in rock

Danny and the Juniors—a recent picture (Neal Hollander Collection)

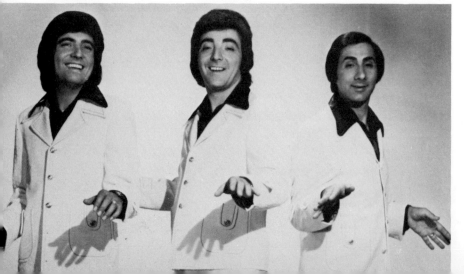

'n' roll history. Two other hit songs by new teenage groups were "Book of Love," the Monotones, and "Little Star," the Elegants.

Even established rock 'n' roll stars like Elvis Presley and Chuck Berry were recording songs about teenagers. "Wear My Ring Around Your Neck" was the first Presley song to actually talk about a teenage fad. When a girl wore her boyfriend's ring around her neck, the couple was going steady. As Elvis pointed out, when you went steady, you wanted the world to know it. Berry's 1958 hits were "Sweet Little Sixteen" and "Johnny B. Goode." Both songs had teenagers as their heroes. The Everly Brothers sang about the double-crossing "Bird Dog," while Buddy Holly paid tribute to "Peggy Sue." The most outrageous rock 'n' roll hit of 1958 was Jerry Lee Lewis's "Great Balls of Fire."

Two unusual hit records in 1958 were "He's Got the Whole World in His Hands," Laurie London, and "Tom Dooley," the Kingston Trio. Both songs came from traditional folk sources. "He's Got the Whole World" is a religious song, while "Tom Dooley" comes from an old Civil War ballad. The Kingston Trio's success with folk material was an early sign of things to come. By the early sixties, folk music had become popular with record buyers. The most interesting cover record of the year was Peggy Lee's "Fever." Her jazzy voice seemed to work well with the sensual lyrics of Little Willie John's song. But in general, 1958 was not a big year for cover records.

The most popular fad of the year, and the one that made the most money, was the hula hoop. Millions of people—young and old—were placing the large plastic hoop over their heads, catching it on one hip, and rotating so that the hoop spun around,

The hula hoop

hardly touching the body. The hula hoops cost pennies to make and sold for about two dollars. Some other fifties' fads were designed for attention and publicity rather than money. One of the better-known ones was called cramming. College students tried to find out how many people they could cram into a phone booth or a Volkswagen Beetle. One national magazine reported that twenty-one male students had fit into a phone booth. Unlike the hula hoop, "cramming" was not an enjoyable excercise. By the end of the year, the fad had passed. At the same time, rock 'n' roll purists were wondering if their music's golden age had not also come and gone.

MAJOR EVENTS OF 1958

Politics and Government

Nikita Khrushchev, Communist Party chief, becomes Premier, thereby gaining full control of the U.S.S.R. government.

Vice President Richard Nixon goes on a goodwill tour of Latin America, but receives an extremely unfriendly welcome from many of the crowds.

"Youth March for Integrated Schools" in Washington, D.C., marks the beginning of student activism.

Congress passes the National Defense Education Act to help improve our schools and raise them to Soviet standards.

Charles de Gaulle returns to power in France as a result of increasing problems in the French-African colony of Algeria.

In the News

There is an increasing number of protests demanding that all nuclear tests be banned.

The John Birch Society, an Extremist right-wing organization, is formed. It is led by Robert Welch.

The first underwater crossing of the North Pole is accomplished by the American submarine *Nautilus*.

The U.S. sends its first successful space satellite, Explorer I, into orbit.

The Arts

The Academy Award for the year's best movie goes to *Gigi.* David Niven wins the best-actor award for his work in *Separate Tables,* while Susan Haywood gets the best-actress Oscar for her moving performance in *I Want to Live.* Other important films include *Black Orpheus, The 400 Blows, The Defiant Ones,* and *Cat on a Hot Tin Roof.*

A new type of comedy becomes increasingly popular. Inspired by the ill-fated Lenny Bruce, a number of satirists become quite well known in the late fifties. These include comedian Mort Sahl and cartoonist Jules Feiffer. This new style of comedy becomes the focus of an entire magazine, *Mad.*

The most popular book of the year is Boris Pasternak's *Dr. Zhivago.* Other important books published in 1958 include *The Affluent Society* by John Kenneth Galbraith, *Lolita* by Vladimir Nabokov, and *Stride Toward Freedom* by Martin Luther King, Jr.

There are several popular Broadway musicals, all of which become movies within a few years. The most popular of these is Lerner and Loewe's *My Fair Lady,* which spawns several hit songs. Another Broadway hit is *Flower Drum Song* with its Oriental flavor. A third musical, *Bye Bye Birdie,* actually spoofs an Elvis-type rock 'n' roll singer.

Television

Crime shows are big in 1958. A new series, "The Untouchables," with Robert Stack, deals with gangsters of the thirties being pursued by the FBI. Narrated by newspaperman Walter Winchell, the show has a documentary style. Other popular crime shows are "77 Sunset Strip" and "Peter Gunn."

Conductor Leonard Bernstein becomes an instant TV personality with his televised classical music concerts. Another popular special show in 1958 in "An Evening with Fred Astaire."

Popular new shows include David Susskind's "Open End" interview show, "Sea Hunt," with Lloyd Bridges as a skindiver, and a new western, "Bat Masterson."

Sports

The New York Yankees win their twenty-fourth American League pennant and their eighteenth World Series.

Stan Musial of the St. Louis Cardinals becomes the eighth player in baseball history to reach the 3,000 hit total.

Floyd Patterson retains his heavyweight title.

The Baltimore Colts defeat the New York Giants in overtime and win the NFL championship.

Fads and Fashion

This is the year of the hula hoop. Originally manufactured in 1957 by the Wham-O Company, this brightly colored plastic hoop, selling for under two dollars, reaches its peak. In 1958, sales climb to an astounding total of $45 million.

Encouraging teenagers to become more clean-cut becomes a fad. Pat Boone writes a book, *Twixt Twelve and Twenty,* which is a best seller. In the book, Boone advises young people on how to deal with the trying years of their lives.

The transistor radio makes its first appearance. Because of space-age advances, kids can listen to rock 'n' roll whenever and wherever they wanted.

Many Americans leave the big cities and move out to the suburbs. The search for better schools and cleaner air leads to an entirely new way of life.

In 1958, chain letters are a big craze. Apparently this particular fad tends to die down and come back. The most popular chain letter at this time deals with buying U.S. savings bonds.

One of the most important fashions of the year is the paisley look. Little amoeba-shaped designs could be seen on shirts, skirts, and even auto seats.

TOP ROCK 'N' ROLL RECORDS OF 1958

Song	Artist	Record Label
All I Have to Do Is Dream	Everly Brothers	Cadence
A Lover's Question	Clyde McPhatter	Atlantic
At the Hop	Danny and the Juniors	ABC Paramount
Bird Dog	Everly Brothers	Cadence

Song	Artist	Record Label
Book of Love	Monotones	Argo
Chantilly Lace	The Big Bopper	Mercury
Do You Want to Dance	Bobby Freeman	Josie
Get a Job	Silhouettes	Ember
Great Balls of Fire	Jerry Lee Lewis	Sun
Hard Headed Woman	Elvis Presley	RCA
I Wonder Why	Dion and the Belmonts	Laurie
Johnny B. Goode	Chuck Berry	Chess
Just a Dream	Jimmy Clanton	Ace
Little Star	The Elegants	APT
Maybe	The Chantels	End
Donna	Richie Valens	Del-Fi
Poor Little Fool	Ricky Nelson	Imperial
Rebel Rouser	Duane Eddy	Jamie
Rock and Roll Is Here to Stay	Danny and the Juniors	ABC Paramount
Rockin' Robin	Bobby Day	Class
Splish Splash	Bobby Darin	Atco
Summer Times Blues	Eddy Cochran	Liberty
Sweet Little Sixteen	Chuck Berry	Chess
Talk to Me, Talk to Me	Little Willie John	King
Tears on My Pillow	Little Anthony and the Imperials	End
Tequila	The Champs	Challenge
To Know Him Is to Love Him	The Teddy Bears	Dare
Twilight Time	The Platters	Mercury
Wear My Ring Around Your Neck	Elvis Presley	RCA
We Belong Together	Robert and Johnny	Old Town
Western Movies	The Olympics	Damon
Yakety Yak	The Coasters	Atlantic
You Cheated	The Shields	Dot
Willie and the Hand Jive	Johnny Otis	Capitol

1959—Year of the Teen Idols

The year began without some of rock 'n' roll's most important artists. Elvis had joined the army, although he did make two records that sold well, "A Big Hunk of Love" and "A Fool Such as I." Little Richard quit rock 'n' roll to become a minister and stopped making records. Jerry Lee Lewis married his teenage cousin and his records were banned. There was a definite feeling of loss among rock 'n' roll fans by the beginning of 1959. But the saddest news of the year came on February 3. Songwriter Don McClean called it "the day the music died." Buddy Holly, Richie Valens, and the Big Bopper had been killed in a plane crash.

Valens had several lively hits with "Come On Let's Go" and "La Bamba," as well as a popular slow song, "Donna." Texas disc jockey J. P. Richardson, also known as the Big Bopper, was riding the success of his novelty hit, "Chantilly Lace," when tragedy struck. Buddy Holly was the most popular of the three deceased performers. He was only twenty-two, but he was recognized as one of the most talented artists of early rock 'n' roll. With the passing of time, Holly's music and legend have become more important than anyone might have imagined.

Now that so many of the most important stars were gone, it was likely that new ones would appear to take their place. Nineteen fifty-nine was to become the year of the teen idols. If you were

174

Two members of the Ricky Nelson fan club present their idol with a cake on his sixteenth birthday. (Courtesy of Kathryn Lance)

good-looking and had a catchy song, you had a chance. Frankie Avalon proved that you did not really have to be a good singer to make hit records. He was only one of many teen idols to reach the charts in 1959.

The city of Philadelphia produced several teen idols. Fabian, Bobby Rydell, and Frankie Avalon all came from Philly's Italian south side. They were all helped tremendously by Dick Clark, who hosted "American Bandstand" from the same city. Frankie Avalon was the first of the three to make it. After reaching the charts with "Dee Dee Dinah" in 1958, Avalon had his biggest year in 1959.

"Venus," which was released in February, became his biggest hit.

Bobby Rydell was a drummer in the same band where Frankie Avalon played trumpet. The group was called Rocco and the Saints. After several flops, Rydell had two successful records in 1959, "Kissin' Time" and "We Got Love." Like most of the other boy idols, he was dark and good-looking. Rydell was even a pretty good singer. He managed to have a few more hits in the early sixties and starred in the movie *Bye Bye Birdie* in 1963.

Fabiano Forte, also known as Fabian, had no musical background at all. Worse, he had very little talent. But Fabian's shortcomings did not stop him from making hits in 1959. It seems that Bob Marcucci, who was Avalon's manager, was looking for another teen idol. As legend has it, Marcucci discovered Fabian sitting on his stoop. There was never any doubt in Marcucci's mind that Fabian would be a star. In his book, *Rock, Roll and Remember*, Dick Clark recalled Marcucci's first description of Fabian:

> "Dick, you know Elvis and Ricky Nelson are really hot. Well, neither of them are doing anything. They're not getting out where the kids can touch them. I figured this out and said to myself, 'I've got to find someone and take him and let him be touched by everybody.' I've got this kid named Fabian. He looks like Ricky Nelson. I want to make him a giant star, put him out on the road where the kids can get close to him."

Bobby Rydell as he looks today (Neal Hollander Collection)

Clark invited Marcucci to bring Fabian to a local hop. According to Clark, Fabian sang ("lip-synched") "I'm a Man," and the young girls went crazy.

The story of Fabian tells a good deal about the state of rock 'n' roll in 1959. The most powerful man in the music business has no objection to promoting a singer who has little or no vocal ability. Clark certainly did not sound like somebody who loved the music. He did not seem to think a great deal of the rock 'n' roll audience's ability to judge which records were good. The public proved that Clark was right. Many records by the teen idols moved to the upper reaches of the charts. In many cases, a singer's good looks were often more important than his voice.

Other teen idols who did well in 1959 were Paul Anka, "Lonely Boy" and "Put Your Head on My Shoulder," and Freddy Cannon, "Tallahassee Lassie." Ricky Nelson had a hit with "Gotta Travel On" after an even bigger year in 1958. Jimmy Clanton was another good-looking teen idol to have hits—"Just a Dream" and "Go Jimmy Go." Of course, some of these superstars actually did make good records. Ricky Nelson, for example, made records that had an authentic rockabilly sound. They were well produced and featured the exciting guitar playing of James Burton.

Many of the new teen idols were really pop singers who were trying to cash in on a fad. The best of these was Bobby Darin. Like Paul Anka, Darin wrote much of his own material. His first three hits were well-done rock 'n' roll records. They were "Splish Splash," "Queen of the Hop," and "Dream Lover." Darin's next release was "Mack the Knife," which was taken from *The Threepenny Opera*. The song was done in a style which was close to Frank Sinatra's big band records. "Mack the Knife" became one of the most popular records of the year. It was selected by the record industry as the best single of the year. Darin discarded rock 'n' roll and continued to have hits in this more traditional style.

The formula for creating a teen idol worked well in 1959. Everyone and his brother seemed to be making a hit record. The award for the silliest hit of the year went to "Kookie" Edd Byrnes for "Kookie Kookie (Lend Me Your Comb)." Byrnes was the star of the popular TV show, "77 Sunset Strip."

Although many listeners felt that these no-talent idols were killing rock 'n' roll, there were a number of good records in 1959.

Connie Francis—one of the few female teen idols (Billy Vera Collection)

There were the early soul hits of Ray Charles, "What'd I Say"; Jackie Wilson, "Lonely Teardrops"; and the Isley Brothers, "Shout." The Drifters introduced their new orchestrated sound with a moving record, "There Goes My Baby." The Coasters continued to turn out catchy and humorous hits—"Charlie Brown" and "Poison Ivy." Two new groups made good records with similar titles. The Falcons' "You're So Fine" and the Fiestas' "So Fine" both became national hits. Other vocal group hits of 1959 were "Sixteen Candles," the Crests, and "A Teenager in Love," Dion and the Belmonts. There were several kinds of instrumental hits in 1959. Santo and Johnny introduced their whining guitar sound in "Sleepwalk"; Dave "Baby" Cortez had a bouncy hit with "The Happy Organ." Martin Denny used a cha-cha beat and sound effects in "Quiet Village," while Ernie Fields brought back the big band era with Glenn Miller's "In the Mood."

In 1959, Lloyd Price had a big year with his commercial New Orleans sound. He had three big hits with "Stagger Lee," "Personality," and "I'm Gonna Get Married." Although these records lacked the bite of his earlier work, they were quite lively and danceable. An unusual hit in 1959 was Wilbert Harrison's hit, "Kansas City." The song had originally been released in 1952 by Little Willie Littlefield as "K. C. Loving." The song was a basic

Chicago blues shuffle. This type of sound was not usually found on the hit parade, but producer Bobby Robinson felt that the song had commercial potential:

> Wilbert Harrison was doing this one man band show in New Jersey. He was using "Kansas City" as a theme song, and it kind of became his trademark. I decided to record him. I was also working with his brothers, Robert and Jimmy, who had a good duet sound. I wanted to record them the same day, so I booked some studio time. I had finished recording his brothers, but Wilbert still hadn't shown up. Just as the musicians were packing up, he walked in. He had a flat tire on the way in and couldn't call. He convinced me that he could do the song real quick. So, I asked the engineer and the musicians if they would stay for another fifteen minutes.
>
> Wilbert played the song once through, and the musicians fell right in. We recorded the song in one take, and I believed that we had a hit. We then recorded the B side, a ballad called "Listen My Darling." The whole session took about fifteen minutes and cost me about fifty dollars—twelve dollars for fifteen minutes of studio time and ten dollars apiece for the musicians. Today, it usually costs thousands of dollars to cut a single.

Back in 1959, many producers were able to invest only a few hundred dollars to make a record. Bobby Robinson sought out

The Fiestas ("Bleecker" Bob Plotnik Collection)

performers who had a distinct vocal style. He then found the right musicians to create the sound he wanted. For example, he credits guitarist Jimmy Spurill for giving "Kansas City" a distinctive sound. The record was one of the best of the year. If only more producers would have concerned themselves with a performer's talent rather than his looks, there would have been better rock 'n' roll in 1959.

The year did not end on a happy note, as the TV quiz show scandals became big news. These shows were extremely popular in the mid-fifties. Some contestants won large sums of money. The best-known winner was Charles Van Doren, who won $129,000 on the show called "21." Van Doren was a university professor from a well-known literary family. When it was disclosed that he was told the answers beforehand, Congress conducted an investigation. A disgraced Van Doren admitted that the shows had been rigged. Other contestants also admitted it. Child actress Patty Duke was one contestant who was given the answers to questions on the "$64,000 Question." The networks apparently had told the contestants that knowing the answers ahead of time would make the shows more entertaining. Van Doren explained his feelings about cheating on the quiz shows to the congressional investigating committee:

> I was almost able to convince myself that it did not matter what I was doing because it was having such a good effect on the national attitude toward teachers, education, and the intellectual life. At the same time, I was winning more money than I ever had or ever dreamed of having. I was able to convince myself that I could make up for it after it was over.

But it was too late to make up for it. The public did not like being deceived. As the television stations canceled most of their quiz shows, the House moved its investigation to other areas of entertainment. By the end of the year, the music business was being closely examined for the practice of paying disc jockeys to push certain records. The word *payola* was coined to describe illegal promotion in the music business. By 1960, the payola scandal shook the young world of rock 'n' roll to its very foundations.

MAJOR EVENTS OF 1959

Politics and Government

In Cuba, Fidel Castro's guerrilla forces capture Havana and overthrow the Batista government. Six months later, the U.S. expresses hostility toward the new Cuban regime.

Alaska is admitted to the Union as the forty-ninth state. A short time later, Hawaii becomes the fiftieth state.

The "kitchen debate" between Nixon and Khrushchev is held in Moscow amid much ill will.

Khrushchev visits the U.S., but is denied admission to Disneyland.

President Eisenhower makes a goodwill tour that encompasses three continents and eleven nations.

In the News

The U.S. selects its first seven astronauts. Among them are Alan Shepard, John Glenn, and Walter Schirra.

The St. Lawrence Seaway opens.

Synthetic penicillin is developed.

The first weather satellite is launched from Cape Canaveral, Florida.

The Arts

Ben Hur wins the Academy Award for the year's best picture; Charlton Heston is the best actor for his performance in the title role. Simone Signoret wins the best-actress Oscar for her role in *Room at the Top*. Other notable films were *The Last Angry Man, Anatomy of a Murder,* and *The Diary of Anne Frank*.

The popularity of classical music has grown during the fifties. By 1959, there are 200 symphony orchestras in the U.S., an increase of 80 percent since the early forties.

Billie Holiday, the era's most revered jazz singer, dies.

Notable books are *Exodus* by Leon Uris, *Advertisements for Myself* by Norman Mailer, and Vance Packard's *The Status Seekers*.

Television

"Your Hit Parade" goes off the air after a ten-year run. The show, which had played the top songs each week, could not adapt its format to rock 'n' roll. Listeners grow tired of hearing plastic performances of their favorite songs. The singers and producers of "Your Hit Parade" are from the old school of popular music, and their time has simply passed.

TV Guide—a weekly handbook of TV programming—has 53 regional editions and a circulation of 65 million.

The most popular programs are detective programs like "Dragnet." Westerns are still doing well, but many comedy programs are losing their sponsors.

Sports

The Los Angeles Dodgers defeat the Chicago White Sox in a six-game World Series.

Swedish heavyweight Ingemar Johansson defeats Floyd Patterson on a technical knockout in the third round. The victory launches Johansson to world's heavyweight champion.

Neale Fraser wins the U.S. Lawn Tennis Association championship. Maria Bueno tops all women in the same event.

The Baltimore Colts, with Johnny Unitas, defeat the New York Giants 31 to 16 and capture the NFL crown.

Fads and Fashion

Health food fads are very big in 1959. "Miracle foods," which supposedly cure everything from cancer to fading youth, included carrot juice, yogurt, grape juice, wheat germ, blackstrap molasses, and brewer's yeast.

A popular activity among teenagers is driving down a main drag, blasting the car radio, and stopping off at the local drive-in for French fries and a Coke.

America seems to go game crazy in 1959. Word games like Scrabble are very popular, as are "doodling" and painting by numbers.

The most popular color of 1959 is purple (sometimes called lavender). Purple sweaters, shirts, skirts, pants, and dresses abound. On many main drags, there is at least one teenager who sports purple hair.

TOP ROCK 'N' ROLL RECORDS OF 1959

Song	Artist	Record Label
A Big Hunk of Love	Elvis Presley	RCA
A Fool Such as I	Elvis Presley	RCA
Almost Grown	Chuck Berry	Chess
Along Came Jones	The Coasters	Atco
Charlie Brown	The Coasters	Atco
Come Softly to Me	The Fleetwoods	Cornerstone
Dream Lover	Bobby Darin	Atco
I'm Gonna Get Married	Lloyd Price	ABC Paramount
I'm Ready	Fats Domino	Imperial
I Want to Be Wanted	Brenda Lee	Decca
Kansas City	Wilbert Harrison	Fury
Lipstick on Your Collar	Connie Francis	MGM
Lonely Boy	Paul Anka	ABC
Lonely Teardrops	Jackie Wilson	Brunswick
Love Potion #9	The Clovers	Atlantic
Personality	Lloyd Price	ABC
Poison Ivy	The Coasters	Atco
Red River Rock	Johnny and the Hurricanes	Warwick
Since I Don't Have You	The Skyliners	Calico
Sixteen Candles	The Crests	Co-ed
Sleep Walk	Santo and Johnny	Canadian-American
Shout	Isley Brothers	RCA
So Fine	The Fiestas	Old Town
Sorry, I Ran All the Way Home	The Impalas	Cub
Stagger Lee	Lloyd Price	ABC
Sweet Nothin's	Brenda Lee	Decca
Tallahassee Lassie	Freddie Cannon	Swann
Teenager in Love	Dion and the Belmonts	Laurie
The Happy Organ	Dave "Baby" Cortez	Clock
There Goes My Baby	The Drifters	Atco
The Right Time	Ray Charles	Atlantic
Tiger	Fabian	Chancellor

Song	Artist	Record Label
Till I Kissed You	Everly Brothers	Cadence
Venus	Frankie Avalon	Cameo
We Got Love	Bobby Rydell	Cameo
What'd I Say	Ray Charles	Atlantic
You're So Fine	The Falcons	Unart

1960—All Shook Up

The payola hearings, which came to a head in 1960, were the biggest scandal in the history of rock. Teenagers were badly "shook up" by the amount of corruption in the record business. They wondered if the records they loved became popular because someone was paying to have them promoted. Adults who disliked rock 'n' roll were now sure that this horrible music was being fed to teens by corrupt disc jockeys who were receiving money and gifts under the table. Actually, payola had been widespread in the music business well before the rock 'n' roll era.

Leaving for the senior prom

185

During the thirties, the live performances of dance bands were broadcast on radio stations throughout the country. At that time, music publishing companies often found it necessary to pay bandleaders to play their songs. Some popular bandleaders simply charged a flat fee for each song they played. This practice of "song plugging" continued into the forties. At that time, records replaced live bands, and disc jockeys now had the power to give records the proper exposure. By the fifties, there were hundreds of new records being released every week. How, then, was a disc jockey to choose which one to promote?

Before the payola hearings, disc jockeys had few guidelines for choosing which records to promote. Therefore, record companies understood that some favor or gift might make a disc jockey more likely to push their product. Payola also took place between distributors and record stores. Retail dealers often received hundreds of free records from certain distributors. In return, dealers were expected to "push" certain records and give them a high rating on weekly popularity polls. These polls were conducted by radio stations and music business trade papers. Therefore, many of these listings were extremely inaccurate.

When a subcommittee of the House of Representatives began questioning people from the music industry, these play-for-pay practices made the headlines. The committee members believed that many of these practices might be illegal. They wondered if it was not a conflict of interest for a disc jockey to own a percentage of a record or a song. Would this disc jockey not be likely to play this record more than one which he did not own? The answer seemed clear. Nevertheless, many disc jockeys were involved in the music business. Alan Freed, for example, had co-written several hits. These included Chuck Berry's "Maybellene" and the Moonglows' "Sincerely." When Freed's radio station asked him to sign a statement that he never took payola, he refused on principle. He was then fired by his station and eventually ruined by charges of payola and tax evasion.

Since Freed was the most important disc jockey during the fifties, it is not surprising that he was such a big target when the payola scandal broke. There could be little doubt that he sometimes promoted a record which he owned a piece of. It was also likely that, at times, Freed accepted gifts from record companies that were trying to promote their product. But, again, these practices had been widespread in the music industry for many years.

By the late fifties, Dick Clark had become far more powerful than any radio disc jockey, including Freed. He had many holdings in the music business, including record companies, song publishing companies, and even a record manufacturing plant. When the payola scandal hit, ABC told Clark to either get rid of his music business interests or leave his job as host of "American Bandstand." By the time Clark was called before the committee, he had sold all of his holdings in the music business. Although he denied ever taking payola, there was some indication that he paid more attention to records in which he had an interest. For example, it was noted that the song "Sixteen Candles" was played only four times on "Bandstand" during a ten-week period. But after Clark's publishing company became part owner of the song, it was played twenty-seven times during the next thirteen weeks. Clark answered these charges by bringing a statistics expert to the hearings with him. This expert had numbers which showed that Clark did not favor his own record interests. Eventually, the committee cleared Clark of any wrongdoing.

The focus of the payola hearings was rock 'n' roll, not the music business in general. Congressmen, like many other adults, could not believe that anyone actually liked this music. It seemed logical that its popularity was due only to illegal payoffs. There was never any mention that rock 'n' roll, even at its worst, was the music which expressed the feelings of the younger generation. Much of the discussion which took place at the payola hearings, therefore, concerned the shortcomings of rock 'n' roll compared with traditional or "good" popular music.

As a result of the hearings, many radio stations switched to top forty programming. Disc jockeys played the programmer's list of the most popular hit singles. Under this system, the announcer's personality became less important, and payola could be reduced. But by 1960, singles only accounted for a small percentage of total record sales. The album or long-play record had become the most popular type of disc. By playing only the most popular singles, stations were ignoring the favorite records of many listeners. Later in the decade, many FM radio stations would begin to turn their attention almost completely to album cuts.

Although 1960 was not the greatest year for rock 'n' roll, there were some good records. These included "Stay," Maurice Williams and the Zodiacs; "New Orleans," Gary U.S. Bonds; "Finger Poppin' Time," Hank Ballard; and "Handy Man," Jimmy Jones. But, in general, the hit parade was dominated by ballads and novelty songs. Even Elvis's big hit, "It's Now or Never," was a remake of an old Italian folk song, "O Sole Mio." Other big hits in 1960 were Percy Faith's instrumental, "Theme from 'A Summer Place' "; Brenda Lee's "I'm Sorry"; "Running Bear," Johnny Preston; and Brian Hyland's "Itsy Bitsy Teenie Weenie Yellow Polka-dot Bikini." Another top record was "The Twist" by Chubby Checker. Originally written and released in 1959 by Hank Ballard, the Twist became a popular dance on "American Bandstand." Two years later, it would become an international craze, and Chubby's record would be an even bigger hit.

There were events outside the music business in 1960 which gave young people reason to hope for a new and better era. Although most of rock 'n' roll's first generation was still too young to vote, there was much excitement over Senator John F. Kennedy. The presidential candidate of the Democratic Party was young and good-looking. He spoke of a new and better world, one with-

Gary U.S. Bonds (Neal Hollander Collection)

out war and poverty. When he accepted the nomination, he said, "The world is changing; the old era is dying; the old ways will not do. . . ."

When Kennedy took over the presidency, he was faced with many problems. A U-2 plane was shot down in April over Russia, and its pilot was accused of being a spy. Soviet Premier Khrushchev walked out of the summit talks in Paris and threatened to attack U.S. bases. There were other serious problems concerning conflicts with Russia over Cuba, just ninety miles away from Florida and under the Communist leadership of Fidel Castro. Americans were so concerned about nuclear attacks that they began building bomb shelters in their basements and backyards.

Young people sincerely believed in this new President, his wife, and their charisma. The Kennedys became the nation's biggest stars. It really did feel like the start of something new. Many rock 'n' rollers of the fifties were now young adults. They had watched the times change with the music. They had witnessed attempts to destroy the music. But it seemed clear that rock 'n' roll could not be destroyed. Some listeners were already looking back to the fifties and buying collections of oldies but goodies. Others were becoming interested in folk music and jazz, which they felt were more mature forms of expression. But for the most part, young people felt that rock 'n' roll would always be the most important music in their lives.

MAJOR EVENTS OF 1960

Politics and Government

Cuba cuts off trade with the U.S. and establishes trade with the Soviet Union. Eisenhower invokes the Monroe Doctrine in an attempt to keep Communism out of the Americas.

Francis Gary Powers, pilot of an American U-2 spy plane, is shot down over Russia, captured, and imprisoned.

Eight million people watch the Kennedy-Nixon debates on TV. Kennedy's charisma and Nixon's "five o'clock shadow" help to seal JFK's victory in the presidential election.

On June 30, seventeen African nations become free and independent countries.

A civil rights bill is passed by Congress to help ensure the voting rights of black citizens in the South.

In the News

Sit-ins become the most popular form of nonviolent protest in the civil rights struggle. By 1960, over 50,000 people have been involved in these demonstrations.

Students for a Democratic Society is formed, thus signaling the beginning of student activism.

After several appeals, convicted murderer and author Caryl Chessman is executed. Protests against capital punishment are heard worldwide.

The Arts

The best picture of the year is *The Apartment*. Burt Lancaster wins the best-actor prize for the title role in *Elmer Gantry*. Elizabeth Taylor captures best-actress honors for her performance in *Butterfield 8*. One of the most popular songs of the year is the theme from the movie *Never on a Sunday*.

Alto saxophone player Ornette Coleman becomes the most controversial jazz musician of 1960. His emotional and free style of improvising causes the biggest debate in jazz circles since Charlie Parker introduced bebop in the forties.

Several popular nonfiction books are concerned with prehistoric life. These include *Hidden America* and *Indians of the High Plains*. Popular novels are *The Mansion* by William Faulkner and *The Devil's Advocate* by Morris L. West.

Important Broadway openings include *Becket* with Anthony Quinn and Laurence Olivier and Lillian Hellman's *Toys in the Attic* with Jason Robards and Maureen Stapleton.

Television

Light comedies do quite well. The most popular of these is "Hennessey," a situation comedy about a Navy doctor starring TV favorite Jackie Cooper.

Jack Paar, host of NBC's "Tonight Show," makes television history by walking out in the middle of the show. The reason for his leaving? Somebody from the station had censored one of his jokes.

Science fiction adds a hit show to the TV season. Rod Serling's "Twilight Zone" tells offbeat and supernatural sci-fi tales, much to the delight of millions of viewers.

By 1960, 90 percent of all American homes have at least one TV set.

Sports

The Pittsburgh Pirates defeat the New York Yankees in a seven-game World Series. Seventy-year-old manager Casey Stengel is fired after a dozen successful years with the Yankees.

Floyd Patterson knocks out Ingemar Johansson and becomes the first heavyweight to regain the championship.

The Philadelphia Eagles defeat the Green Bay Packers 17 to 13 for the NFL championship.

Fads and Fashion

An increasing number of American families build bomb shelters in their basements and backyards. These underground shelters—supplied with food, water, and filtered air—are built to protect families in case of nuclear attacks.

According to a survey taken by the U.S. Census, three out of five families are living in their own homes.

Statistics show that marriage in the new decade is more popular than ever before, but so is divorce.

The eating habits of Americans are leaning more toward snacks and fast foods. In 1960, a billion pounds of hot dogs and 532 million pounds of potato chips are consumed.

TOP ROCK 'N' ROLL RECORDS OF 1960

Song	Artist	Record Label
Angel Baby	Rosie and the Originals	Highland
Cathy's Clown	Everly Brothers	Warner Brothers

Song	Artist	Record Label
Chain Gang	Sam Cooke	RCA
Fannie Mae	Buster Brown	Fire
Finger Poppin' Time	Hank Ballard and the Midnighters	King
Gee Whiz	Carla Thomas	Atlantic
Georgia on My Mind	Ray Charles	Atlantic
Good Timing	Jimmy Jones	Cub
Handy Man	Jimmy Jones	Cub
I'm Sorry	Brenda Lee	MGM
Let's Go, Let's Go, Let's Go	Hank Ballard and the Midnighters	King
Money	Barrett Strong	Anna
New Orleans	Gary U.S. Bonds	Le Grand
Only the Lonely	Roy Orbison	Monument
Save the Last Dance for Me	The Drifters	Atco
Stay	Maurice Williams and the Zodiacs	Herald
The Twist	Chubby Checker	Parkway
Walk Don't Run	The Venturas	Delton
Wild One	Bobby Rydell	Cameo
Wonderful World	Sam Cooke	RCA
You Got What It Takes	Marv Johnson	United Artists
You Talk Too Much	Joe Jones	Roulette

11

1961—Dedicated to the One I Love

Rock 'n' roll made a comeback in 1961. There were some new faces and new sounds to go along with the new decade. The Motown sound was becoming popular with hits like "Shop Around," the Miracles, and "Mr. Postman," the Marvellettes. These records were in the tradition of earlier R&B, but the newer sounds were more sophisticated. Instead of using only a few rhythm instruments, record producers now backed up singers with large orchestras. In some cases, the combination of a rock beat and violins led to memorable records. Two of the best were performed by Ben E. King, formerly of the Drifters, and produced by Phil Spector. "Spanish Harlem," released in January, combined King's strong voice with a large orchestra and a haunting steel drum. The record was one of the best and most popular of the year. King's second solo hit, "Stand By Me," was another good record that became a R&B classic. It was covered many times by a number of performers, including a young boxer named Muhammad Ali.

Not all of the successful rock 'n' roll records of 1961 were recorded with lush orchestras. There were a number of popular songs in updated versions of older styles. One of the biggest records of the year was Bobby Lewis's "Tossin' and Turnin'." It featured a snappy beat, a full horn sound, and a lively vocal performance by Lewis. An even livelier hit was Gary U.S. Bonds' "A

Quarter to Three." Bonds' raunchy voice was combined with a growling tenor sax for one of the most danceable and high-spirited records of the year.

There were several other hits in a lively and humorous vein. Three of the most popular came out of New Orleans, a city known for these kinds of records. Ernie K. Doe's "Mother-in-Law" was about the singer's least favorite person. On the other hand, Chris Kenner's "I Like It Like That," and Lee Dorsey's "Ya Ya" had words that seemed to have no meaning. This was not unusual. Many clever writers had managed to turn a catchy nonsense phrase into a hit record. Bobby Robinson, who co-wrote "Ya Ya" with Lee Dorsey, described how the song came about:

> I was down in New Orleans, and I wanted to record Lee Dorsey. I knew he was a great singer, but he didn't have any original material. I only had a couple of days before I had to leave, and we were kind of stuck for a tune. Well, we were sitting on Lee's front porch trying to figure something out. Suddenly, I heard these kids out in the yard playing a game. They were clapping their hands and singing "Sittin' on my ya-ya, sittin' on my ya-ya." I said to Lee, "Listen to what those kids are singing. I think there's something there that we can use." That night we were still trying to figure out what to do with that little phrase. I didn't want to say "Sittin' on my ya-ya" so I tried to make a little story out of it. It was about a guy waiting for his girl. I went, "Sittin' here la-la, waitin' for my ya-ya," and Lee went "Uh-huh, uh-huh." The next two lines just seemed to flow after that. "It may sound funny, but I don't believe she's coming . . . " Again, Lee answered, "Uh-huh, uh-huh." The next day we went in and recorded the tune, and it became a top ten hit. . . .

Another hit on Robinson's Fury label was "Every Beat of My Heart" by the Pips. Seventeen-year-old Gladys Knight, her brother, and two first cousins were orginally a gospel group that sang at various churches in Atlanta under a different name. But at night, the Pips worked at R&B clubs in another part of town. In late April, an Atlanta DJ asked Robinson to listen to a demo of the group singing Johnny Otis's "Every Beat of My Heart." Robinson was so impressed he immediately flew the group and three other members of the Knight family to New York. The song was re-

Gladys Knight and the Pips at their first New York recording session with producer Bobby Robinson (*to the left of Gladys*) (Courtesy of Bobby Robinson)

corded the following night and became the first of many hits for the group. Like many popular black acts, the Pips have softened their sound in the seventies. But on her first records—"Every Beat of My Heart" and "Letter Full of Tears"—Gladys showed herself to be one of the great female R&B singers of her generation.

Another gospel-influenced group to make its recording debut in 1961 was the Impressions. The leader of this Chicago-based group, Curtis Mayfield, wrote the song, "Gypsy Woman"—the first of a long series of hits for the Impressions. The unique high harmony sound of the group has been widely copied by a number of popular performers, including the Bee Gees. Mayfield has gone on to have a successful career as a solo singer, writer, and producer. Originally, Mayfield and the Impressions backed up Jerry Butler, a rich-voiced gospel-style singer. Together with Mayfield, Butler wrote "He Will Break Your Heart." The song, which featured the Impressions singing background, revived Butler's career in early 1961. But the biggest hit by a Chicago R&B singer that year was

"Raindrops" by Dee Clark. It was one of the most popular records in a year that had many hits in authentic R&B styles.

Elvis's popularity seemed to be slipping in 1961, although he did have one hit with "Little Sister." Roy Orbison, who also originally recorded on the Sun label, joined Elvis on the charts with "Runnin' Scared." Orbison sang in kind of a dramatic rockabilly style, and his sound was quite popular in the early sixties. Neil Sedaka, a songwriter with a high-pitched voice, had a hit with "Calendar Girl" in January. Del Shannon, who had an even higher voice, did well with "Runaway" in April. Dion Dimucci, now singing without the Belmonts, had a smash with "Runaround Sue." The song was especially popular in New York and Philadelphia. Ricky Nelson had his biggest hit in 1961. "Travelin' Man" was originally sent to Sam Cooke, who turned it down. But Nelson, who had gone through a dry spell, was looking for a hit tune. When songwriter Jerry Fuller suggested that he do "Travelin' Man," Nelson knew the song would be a smash. His follow-up record, "Hello Mary Lou," was also a big hit.

Nineteen sixty-one was not the greatest year for vocal groups, although there was an interesting variety of successful records by groups. Two of the better ballads of the year were "My True Story," the Jive Five, and "Daddy's Home," Shep and the Limelights. A popular up-tempo group record was the Marcels' novelty version of the old standard, "Blue Moon." The record featured a stuttering bass voice who sang, "Bomp bomp-a-bomp-a-bomp-a bom bomp, bop-a bomp-a-bom bomp, ding-a-dong ding, blue moon." Another group, Little Caesar and the Romans, sold a lot of records of a slow doo-wop song called "Those Oldies but Good-

Dion then and now (Neal Hollander Collection)

The Five Royales (Billy Vera Collection)

ies." The group sang in a 1956 style, while the lyrics longed for the loves and the songs of the past. As early as 1961, people were thinking about the fifties as those good old days gone by.

Although many radio stations switched to top forty programming in the early sixties, they often used gimmicks which originated in the fifties. Many fast-talking DJs were reading dedications before each song. Kids would request hit songs and dedicate them to their steadies or friends. The jockeys simply read them off with machine-gun speed before each number. One of the most popular songs of the year was the Shirelles' "Dedicated to the One I Love." But even this song came from an early fifties R&B hit by the Five Royales.

A number of hit records were successful attempts to create new dance crazes. Chubby Checker was still riding high with "The Pony" and "The Twist," while the Dovells got kids to dance "The Bristol Stomp." By 1962 the Twist would become an international fad, and dance records would dominate the charts. But a new fad seemed to be sweeping the country in 1961—it was called Kennedy-watching.

The nation was completely taken by its new young President and his glamorous wife. At his inauguration, Kennedy acknowledged that "the torch has been passed to a new generation." The accent of the new administration was definitely on youth. The word that was most often used to describe Kennedy was charisma. Young people, especially, wanted to follow his lead, The new President stressed physical fitness and moral commitment. He was also extremely popular as an international figure and was better liked in foreign countries than any recent President. The world was also enchanted by the new First Lady. She spoke to people in their native languages and won their affections. She also became the most important figure in the world of fashion. If Jackie wore a new style, it quickly became the latest rage.

In spite of growing tensions with Cuba and Russia, people had the sense that things would work out. There was a great feeling of confidence in the new administration, particularly among young people. At the same time, the older generation was starting to be influenced by this new youthful outlook. They were even beginning to respond to the primitive beat of rock 'n' roll. By the following year, millions of adults were dancing to the very music they used to hate.

MAJOR EVENTS OF 1961

Politics and Government

The United States ends diplomatic relations with Cuba. The American government now considers Cuba a Russian satellite and a part of the international Communist movement.

The Twenty-third Amendment to the U.S. Constitution is approved. Citizens of Washington, D.C., may now vote in presidential elections.

The Peace Corps is created by President Kennedy. Its purpose is to recruit young people to serve in the underdeveloped countries of the world and to improve the quality of life in those places.

The Russians close the border between East and West Berlin in order to stop emigration to the West. The U.S. protests and sends troops to West Berlin.

In the News

Russia orbits the first man in space. Major Yuri A. Gagarin circles the earth in 108 minutes.

The U.S. sends commander Alan B. Shepard into space on a suborbital flight of 115 miles. The trip takes fifteen minutes.

General Douglas MacArthur returns to the Philippines to celebrate their fifteenth year of independence. He delivers his famous farewell speech which contains the line, "I shall return."

Adolf Eichmann, former Nazi chief of Jewish affairs, is captured by the Israeli secret service. He is charged with crimes against humanity and the Jewish people. An Israeli court sentences Eichmann to death.

The Arts

The best motion picture of the year is *West Side Story*. Sophia Loren wins the best-actress award for her moving performance in *Two Women*. The best-actor award goes to Maximilian Schell for his role in *Judgment at Nuremberg*. Other notable films include *The Hustler* and *La Dolce Vita*.

The leading U.S. school of art is Abstract Expressionism.

Popular books of 1961 include *Catcher in the Rye* and *Frannie and Zooey* by J. D. Salinger. These books show an acute understanding of the emotional problems of growing up. Another popular book is John Steinbeck's *The Winter of Our Discontent*.

Two successful Broadway plays of 1961 are *How to Succeed in Business Without Really Trying* and *Purlie*.

Television

The most acclaimed TV show of the year is "MacBeth," presented by the Hallmark Hall of Fame.

TV captures a rare and beautiful moment as the aging poet Robert Frost reads a poem at the inauguration of President John F. Kennedy.

News is becoming more linked with TV than any other medium. Instead of merely reading a paper, viewers can actually witness events as they happen around the world.

Sports

The New York Yankees defeat the Cincinnati Reds 4 games to 1, and win their nineteenth World Series championship.

Yankee slugger Roger Maris hits 61 home runs and breaks Babe Ruth's mark of 60 set in 1927.

Floyd Patterson knocks out Ingemar Johansson in the sixth round to retain his heavyweight title.

The Green Bay Packers shut out the New York Giants 37 to 0 to win the NFL championship.

Fads and Fashion

Young people of the early sixties are more socially conscious than teenagers of the fifties. They are now interested in such issues as race relations, banning the bomb, poverty, and capital punishment. Many students participate in demonstrations, while thousands join the Peace Corps.

A big college fad in 1961 is to flock to the beaches of Fort Lauderdale, Florida, during Easter vacation. The beer flows as freely as the salt water and sunshine, and this break from school becomes one of the year's social highlights.

The new trends in fashions are set by the good-looking President and his stylish young wife. In fact, Jackie is considered the best-dressed woman in America, and her tastes in clothing will dominate the women's fashion world for the next few years.

TOP ROCK 'N' ROLL RECORDS OF 1961

Song	Artist	Record Label
A Little Bit of Soap	The Jarmels	Laurie
A Quarter to Three	Gary U.S. Bonds	Le Grand
Blue Moon	The Marcels	Colpix
Calendar Girl	Neil Sedaka	RCA
Crying	Roy Orbison	Monument

Song	Artist	Record Label
Daddy's Home	Shep and the Limelights	Hull
Dedicated to the One I Love	The Shirelles	Sceptor
Every Beat of My Heart	Gladys Knight and the Pips	Fury
Gypsy Woman	Impressions	ABC
Hats Off to Larry	Del Shannon	Big Top
Hello Mary Lou	Ricky Nelson	Imperial
He Will Break Your Heart	Jerry Butler	Vee Jay
Hit the Road Jack	Ray Charles	ABC
I Like It Like That	Chris Kenner	Instant
Letter Full of Tears	Gladys Knight and the Pips	Fury
Let's Twist Again	Chubby Checker	Parkway
Mamma Said	The Shirelles	Sceptor
Mother-in-Law	Ernie K. Doe	Minit
My True Story	The Jive Five	Beltone
Please Mr. Postman	The Marvellettes	Tamla
Raindrops	Dee Clark	Vee Jay
Runaround Sue	Dion	Laurie
Runaway	Del Shannon	Big Top
School Is Out	Gary U.S. Bonds	Le Grand
Shop Around	The Miracles	Tamla
Spanish Harlem	Ben E. King	Atco
Stand By Me	Ben E. King	Atco
The Pony	Chubby Checker	Parkway
Those Oldies but Goodies	Little Caesar and the Romans	Del Fi
Tossin' and Turnin'	Bobby Lewis	Beltone
Travelin' Man	Ricky Nelson	Imperial
What's Your Name	Don and Juan	Big Top
Ya Ya	Lee Dorsey	Fury

1962—The Twist and Other Dance Crazes

An unusual thing happened at the end of 1961. A popular teenage dance, the Twist, became a worldwide craze. The original recording of "The Twist" was by Hank Ballard and the Midnighters in 1959. But the version that became popular was by Chubby Checker—an overweight chicken plucker from Philadelphia. The dance was very popular on "American Bandstand" in 1960 and 1961. Although the music and beat of the Twist were similar to many older R&B songs, the dance was hailed as an innovation. Checker not only sang, he actually danced the Twist while

A twist party circa 1962

202

Joey Dee (Neal Hollander Collection)

he performed. After an appearance on the Ed Sullivan show in late 1961, Chubby and his dance were more popular than ever. By the beginning of 1962, many famous socialites were packing a small New York club called the Peppermint Lounge in order to be part of this new craze.

The band at the Peppermint Lounge was Joey Dee and the Starlighters. Their record, "The Peppermint Twist," was topping the charts, and well-known celebrities were paying off doormen and maitre d's to get closer to the club's tiny dance floor. Some of the important bodies who danced at the Peppermint Lounge were Greta Garbo, Ambassador Adlai Stevenson, playwright Tennessee Williams, and the Duke of Bedford. Once all of these famous people began doing the Twist, millions of adult Americans followed. The craze quickly spread to other parts of the world, and soon there were Twist shoes, Twist pajamas, Twist chairs, and even Twist hairdos.

The tremendous popularity of the Twist seemed to indicate that the older generation had now accepted rock 'n' roll. There were a number of popular Twist records in 1962 including "Twistin' the Night Away," Sam Cooke; "Dear Lady Twist," Gary U.S. Bonds; the instumental "Soul Twist," King Curtis; "Slow Twistin'," Dee Dee Sharp; and the best Twist record of all, "Twist and Shout" by the Isley Brothers. Record companies sometimes repackaged older releases that had a similar beat into Twist albums. One such LP, *Do the Twist with Ray Charles,* became a top-selling album.

The Twist, like most other rock dances, required that the partners stand apart and not touch. The dancers seemed totally concerned with their own movements, and it was often difficult to tell who was dancing with whom on a crowded floor of Twisters. Although many rock dances were invented by the young dancers themselves, others—like the Twist—contained the instructions in the lyrics to the song. Chubby Checker, now a million dollars richer, explained the movements involved in the Twist: "The first position of the stance is like a boxer's. Then you move your hips like you're wiping yourself with a towel. Your body goes back and forth in one direction and your hands go in the other direction."

By the middle of 1962, the Twist was so widely accepted by adults that many kids considered the dance out of fashion. At the same time, some authorities agreed with Chubby Checker's comment that Africans had been doing a dance like the Twist for years. A number of bans followed. Egypt's Premier Nasser forbade his countrymen to Twist, while Indonesia's President Sukarno actually arrested people caught Twisting. There were also some bans in this country. Tampa, Florida, forbade Twisting in its community centers, while several Catholic schools and parishes banned the dance on the grounds of bad taste. For the most part, however,

Dee Dee Sharp (Courtesy of *Record World* magazine)

Little Eva (Neal Hollander
Collection)

the Twist became part of adult dancing, just as rock 'n' roll (by
now it was called rock) had found its place in the mainstream of
American popular music.

Because of the enormous success of the Twist, record companies
were trying to identify performers with new dances. The Philadelphia label that released the Twist, Cameo-Parkway, was behind
many of these hits, including, "Wah Watusi," the Orlons;
"Mashed Potato Time" and "Ride," Dee Dee Sharp; and "The
Bristol Stomp," the Dovells. Chubby Checker followed "The
Twist" and "Let's Twist Again" with several other popular dance
records—"The Fly," "The Popeye" and "Limbo Rock." Another
popular dance record in 1962 was "The Locomotion" by Little
Eva.

There were many other dances which were popular in different
parts of the country. The most successful were those that got seen
on national TV shows like "American Bandstand." To outsiders,
many of these dances looked the same. But many teenagers took
great pride in knowing the many different dances which could be
done to a rock beat. One hit single, "Do You Love Me . . . (Now
That I Can Dance)," told of the importance of knowing *all* the
new steps. As rock scholar Carl Belz points out, "The question of

old dances versus new dances became a central issue in determining which listeners were most up-to-date."

There were some other popular rock records, aside from the dance hits, in 1962. Clyde McPhatter, former lead singer of the Dominoes and the Drifters, had his biggest solo hit with "Lover Please." Sam Cooke made one of his best popular records, "Bring It on Home to Me." Ray Charles did well with his up-tempo, "Unchain My Heart," while Booker T. and the MG's hit with a blues-based instrumental, "Green Onions." Other memorable records were Gene Chandler's "Duke of Earl"; "You Beat Me to the Punch," Mary Wells; "Let Me In," the Exciters; and Candy Clark's "Party Lights."

A new group, the Four Seasons, began having huge hits in 1962. The group was similar to other East Coast white groups, with one important difference—the unique ultrahigh voice of lead singer Frankie Valli. The group had worked in small New Jersey clubs as the Four Lovers. In 1961, they got involved with producer Bob Crewe, who helped them develop their sound. Shortly after signing with Vee Jay Records, the group's first single, "Sherry," was released. Within a few weeks, the song became a number one hit. The group's follow-up record, "Big Girls Don't Cry," also reached the top of the charts. The Four Seasons had a series of hits up until the early seventies.

Frankie Valli and the Four Seasons (Neal Hollander Collection)

In 1966, Valli began recording as a solo performer, in addition
to his records with the group. He had his first big hit in 1967 with
"Can't Take My Eyes Off of You" and has been a popular
recording artist through the seventies. His later hits include the
title song from the movie *Grease.*

There were also some interesting developments outside the
music business in 1962. America launched its first man into deep
space. Richard Nixon was defeated in his bid to become governor
of California. There were problems in the Far East, the Near East,
and in neighboring Cuba. The arms race with Russia was still on,
as the U.S. resumed nuclear testing in the Pacific. The tests were
the first of this kind since 1958. Former First Lady Eleanor Roose-
velt died, after devoting much of her life to fighting for civil liber-
ties. A more untimely death was that of actress Marilyn Monroe
from an apparent overdose of sleeping pills. In spite of all these
events, 1962 was a relatively calm year. But for Chubby Checker,
Joey Dee, and the owners of the Peppermint Lounge, there would
never be a magical year like the one that had just passed.

MAJOR EVENTS OF 1962

Politics and Government

East-West conference on banning nuclear weapons—which had
begun in 1958—ends without reaching any decision on nuclear
testing.

President Kennedy sends 4,000 troops into Thailand to ward off
Communist forces.

Francis Gary Powers—the American U-2 pilot who was shot
down over Russia—is exchanged for a Soviet spy serving time in
the U.S.

President Kennedy announces that the Soviet Union has nuclear
missiles and air bases in Cuba. He orders American ships to blockade Cuba. Several days later, the Soviets begin removing the missiles and the U.S. ends the blockade.

JFK, a long-time fighter for civil rights, bans discrimination in
federal housing.

In the News

By a democratic vote, Algeria gains independence after 132 years of colonization and seven and a half years of war with France.

John Glenn becomes America's first man to orbit the earth. He circles the planet three times in four hours and fifty-six minutes.

Mrs. Kennedy visits Rome and has an audience with Pope John. She also makes stops in London, India, and Pakistan.

Steel companies' prices go up. After President Kennedy denounces these increases, the companies roll back their prices.

The Arts

The Oscar for the year's best picture goes to *Lawrence of Arabia.* Gregory Peck is the best actor for his role in *To Kill a Mockingbird,* and Anne Bancroft wins best-actress laurels for *The Miracle Worker.* Other notable films are *Lolita, Days of Wine and Roses,* and *Last Year at Marienbad.*

The New York Philharmonic Orchestra gives its last concert in Carnegie Hall before moving to Lincoln Center.

The New York City Ballet Company becomes the first American dance troupe to dance at Moscow's Bolshoi Theater. Later in the year, the Bolshoi Ballet comes to the U.S., where many critics rate its choreography as old-fashioned.

Notable plays of 1962 include *The Caretaker* by Harold Pinter, *A Thousand Clowns,* and *The Affair.*

Television

The biggest event in TV is Telstar—a satellite that transmits signals over oceans and continents. In July, Telstar flashes its first pictures from Britain and France to TV screens in the U.S. This represents a new era in communications and reporting of live events all over the world.

TV shows its greatest ingenuity by reporting orbital space flights as they happen. The flight by astronauts Glenn, Schirra, and Carpenter is watched by 135 million viewers.

Sports

The New York Yankees defeat the San Francisco Giants in six games to win the World Series.

Los Angeles Dodger shortstop Maury Wills sets an all-time record by stealing 104 bases.

Sonny Liston wins the heavyweight title by knocking out Floyd Patterson two minutes and six seconds into the first round in what the papers had predicted would be "the fight of the decade."

The Green Bay Packers win the NFL title by beating the New York Giants for the second year in a row. This year, the Giants make it a game, losing by a score of 16 to 7.

Fads and Fashion

Compact cars like the Plymouth Valiant and the Ford Falcon become increasingly popular. The safety belt becomes standard equipment in all 1962 cars.

Women's fashions are again strongly influenced by Jackie Kennedy. After her trip to India, tunics, rajah coats, and split skirts become popular. Other fashionable women's clothing include pea-jackets, knee-length fitted shirts, and bouffant ballgowns.

Many men wear brown suits with wider lapels. Olive green is another popular color in hats, sweaters, and shirts. A new kind of plaid material called "madras" or "bleeding madras" becomes the summer rage in both men's and women's fashions.

TOP ROCK 'N' ROLL RECORDS OF 1962

Song	Artist	Record Label
Any Day Now	Chuck Jackson	Wand
Baby Its You	The Shirelles	Sceptor
Beachwood 4-5789	The Marvellettes	Tamla
Big Girls Don't Cry	The Four Seasons	Vee Jay
Breaking Up Is Hard to Do	Neil Sedaka	RCA
Bring It on Home to Me	Sam Cooke	RCA
Chains	The Cookies	Dimension
Cryin' in the Rain	Everly Brothers	Warner Brothers
Dear Lady Twist	Gary U.S. Bonds	Le Grand

Song	Artist	Record Label
Don't Play That Song	Ben E. King	Atco
Do You Love Me	The Contours	Gordy
Duke of Earl	Gene Chandler	Vee Jay
Green Onions	Booker T and the MG's	Stax
He's a Rebel	The Crystals	Philles
I Know	Barbara George	Saturn
I Need Your Lovin'	Don Gardner and Dee Dee Ford	Fire
Let Me In	The Sensations	Argo
The Locomotion	Little Eva	Dimension
Lover Please	Clyde McPhatter	Atlantic
Mashed Potato Time	Dee Dee Sharp	Cameo
On Broadway	The Drifters	Atlantic
Party Lights	Claudine Clark	Chancellor
Peppermint Twist	Joey Dee and the Starlighters	Roulette
Release Me	Little Ester Phillips	Lenox
She Cried	Jay and the Americans	United Artists
Sherry	The Four Seasons	Vee Jay
Slow Twistin'	Chubby Checker	Parkway
Smokey Places	The Corsairs	Tuff
Soldier Boy	The Shirelles	Sceptor
Soul Twist	King Curtis	Enjoy
Stormy Monday Blues	Bobby "Blue" Bland	Duke
Stubborn Kind of Fellow	Marvin Gaye	Motown
The Bristol Stomp	The Dovells	Cameo
The One Who Really Loves You	Mary Wells	Motown
Twist and Shout	Isley Brothers	Wand
Unchain My Heart	Ray Charles	ABC
Up on the Roof	The Drifters	Atlantic
Uptown	The Crystals	Philles
Wah Watusi	The Orlons	Cameo
You'll Lose a Good Thing	Barbara Lynn	Jamie

13

1963—A Turning Point

The events of 1963 represented a turning point in the music arena and in the world in general. For one thing, the adult world was definitely taking the young generation a lot more seriously than it had in the past. With the popularity of the Twist came an increasing interest in the ideas, styles, and language of the young. Most of rock 'n' roll's first generation was out of high school and either in college or working. The teenagers of the fifties were the young adults of the sixties, and their tastes were of great interest to advertisers, fashion designers, politicians, and record company executives.

Because the rock audience was growing, there was room for a number of new artists. Many of the old favorites from the mid-fifties were either out of the music business or unsuccessfully trying to make new hits. Times were changing, and new voices were being heard. Motown artists like Smokey Robinson and Marvin Gaye were coming into their own in 1963. But the Detroit company's biggest record was by a blind thirteen-year-old singer. Little Stevie Wonder's live record of "Fingertips" was one of the top ten records of the year. His breathless style of singing and harmonica playing became one of the most beloved sounds of the era. If someone asked what soulful singing was, he was told to listen to a Stevie Wonder record. As great as Little Stevie was, few people could have predicted that he would become one of the outstanding geniuses of popular music by the time he reached his early twenties.

Soul music was coming into its own by 1963, and Stevie Wonder was not the only soul performer to make his debut in 1963. The late Otis Redding recorded two slow ballads, "These Arms of Mine" and "Pain in My Heart" in a style that was strongly influenced by Sam Cooke. But Otis' voice was both thicker and raspier than Sam's. In time, Otis evolved his own style and he became the most important soul singer of the mid-sixties. His most popular song was "(Sittin' on) The Dock of the Bay," which was released in December of 1967; just a few days after his death in a plane crash.

Another important soul singer who made his debut in 1963 was Wilson Pickett. Formerly the lead singer of the Falcons, Pickett received some attention with his first solo record, "If You Need Me." Singing in a style that was raspier than Redding's, Pickett became one of the most successful soul singers of the mid-sixties. His hits included "In the Midnight Hour," "Mustang Sally," and "Funky Broadway."

Women were also making their mark on the new soul sounds in 1963. Mary Wells did well with "Two Lovers," while Martha Reeves and the Vandellas created excitement with "Heat Wave." Inez Fox did a moving version of "Mockingbird," which James Taylor and Carly Simon somehow turned into a happy song. Barbara Lewis's "Hello Stranger" and Ruby and the Romantics' "Our

Martha and the Vandellas—one of several successful Motown acts in 1963 (Neal Hollander Collection)

Dionne Warwick (Neal Hollander Collection)

Day Will Come" were soulful ballads with just a hint of bossa nova rhythm. Nineteen sixty-three was also the year of Dionne Warwick's first releases. Her first two hits, "Don't Make Me Over" and "Anyone Who Had a Heart," were in a more soulful style than her later work. Perhaps this was because of a change of direction by her songwriters, Burt Bacharach and Hal David. Like many successful black singers, Dionne softened her style to suit the pop tastes of Las Vegas audiences.

The most popular new female performer in 1963 was Leslie Gore, with three huge hits—"It's My Party," "Judy's Turn to Cry," and "You Don't Own Me." Leslie was a seventeen-year-old high school student when she was discovered by Quincy Jones of Mercury Records. All of her hits were concerned with teenage love. Leslie had a young pleading sound which worked well with the lyrics she sang. Unfortunately, she only had one big year in the record business.

Another new female performer was Diana Ross, lead singer of the Supremes. She had a young and sexy sound which became enormously popular in the mid-sixties. "When the Lovelight Starts

Lesley Gore (Neal Hollander Collection)

Shining Through His Eyes" was only a moderate hit compared with many of the group's later records. In 1964, the group had its first number one hit, "Where Did Our Love Go." They then had five straight top records in a row. During the next five years, the Supremes had twelve number one hits. These numbers are unmatched by a female group in the history of popular music. By the time Diana Ross left the group in 1969, she was the most popular female recording artist in the business. Although Motown president Berry Gordy deserves much credit for developing and packaging the group, he could not match the Supremes' success with his other female acts. In fact, few of the popular girl groups were able to extend their magic beyond one or two hits.

The most popular girl group of the early sixties was the Shirelles. They had a string of hits dating back to 1958 and were still going strong in 1963 with "Foolish Little Girl." Their sound had influenced many other groups, many of whom had great success in 1963. Some of the important girl group records of the year were, "Sally Go Round the Roses," the Jaynettes; "Da Doo Ron Ron," the Crystals; and "Be My Baby," the Ronettes. Unfortunately, most of the girl groups faded from the hit parade by the following year. Their place was taken over by the Beatles and other groups that were part of the British invasion of 1964.

Another rock style that became popular in 1963 was surf music. Two California groups—Jan and Dean and the Beach Boys—made records that reflected the year-round sun and surf scene in southern California. Many of the songs concerned cars, since there was a shortage of public transportation in the West. Many kids started driving at a very young age, and cars became a way of life. The Beach Boys, with songs like "Surfin' U.S.A." and "Little Deuce Coupe," reflected this California lifestyle. Their voices were high pitched and clean-cut. Some of their harmonies sounded more like a forties pop group than rock 'n' roll. But the music had a driving feel that was borrowed from Chuck Berry. The overall sound of the Beach Boys seemed to go well with driving down the highway. Their lyrics seemed to capture the attitude of many young people at that time. Although the group grew more musically complex in the late sixties, live audiences still responded most to the old surfing and car songs.

Although rock was going in new directions, many young people were turning their attention to folk music. There were hootenanny shows on television, and performers like the Christie Minstrels and the Kingston Trio were doing quite well with their commercial folk sounds. But a more serious folk artist, Bob Dylan, was gaining a good deal of attention. Dylan was a gifted poet, but his rough singing style was considered too crude for the hit parade. It took a smooth-sounding folk trio called Peter, Paul, and Mary to turn a Dylan song into a commercial hit. In fact, the group did well with two of Dylan's tunes—"Blowin' in the Wind" and "Don't Think Twice, It's All Right." The words to both songs were closer to poetry than most popular lyrics. "Blowin' in the Wind" was a social protest song that called for an end to war and racial prejudice. But something in the song implied that the writer believed that things would have to get worse before they got better.

On November 22, 1963, President Kennedy was killed by an assassin's bullet. The shock was overwhelming. To the young people of this nation, Kennedy had symbolized hope for a better future. But his death seemed to indicate that times would soon be even more violent. Several days later, a nation watched while suspected assassin Lee Harvey Oswald was murdered by a man who pushed his way through a crowd. The experience of witnessing a second killing on national TV was more than most people could take. But there were to be more brutal assassinations before the decade was over.

The early rock 'n' roll years closed on a note of tragedy. Life seemed to become more complicated in the sixties, and so did the new rock music. Young people were more complex, and they wanted a popular music that would suit their new moods. They got what they wanted. Protest music, art-rock, psychedelic music, all were popular in the sixties. Although they survive in some form today, an increasing number of performers and listeners are turning to an older and more basic form of music. It is not a music that bombards the senses or provokes complicated thoughts. It is a simple and direct music that makes you feel good—it is good old rock 'n' roll.

MAJOR EVENTS OF 1963

Politics and Government

The U.S., the U.S.S.R., and Great Britain sign a nuclear test ban. This prohibits the exploding of atomic devices in the atmosphere. The agreement seems to lead to an easing of cold war tensions.

In Alabama, black students are admitted to public schools. Federal troops induce Governor George Wallace to step down from schoolhouse steps as three students go to classes.

The struggle continues in Southeast Asia to contain Communist countries. South Vietnam is an important trouble spot, as the Vietcong take an increasing number of American lives.

Integration leaders organize a massive "March on Washington" in an attempt to ensure passage of the civil rights bill. Dr. Martin Luther King addresses some 200,000 people at an orderly gathering at Lincoln Memorial. He states: "One day this nation will rise up and live out the true meaning of its creed—'we hold these truths to be self-evident, that all men are created equal.' "

Communist China and Russia are tense over questions concerning Cuba. The Kremlin is cool to a Chinese call for a world Communist meeting.

John F. Kennedy is shot by an assassin on November 22. Vice President Lyndon B. Johnson assumes the presidency.

In the News

The sixteenth Baptist Church of Birmingham, Alabama, is bombed on September 15, killing four girls as they attend Sunday school. The same day two Birmingham black youths are fatally shot.

A newspaper strike in New York City lasts 114 days.

Mariner II brings back the first accurate piece of information about the planet Venus. Venus's 800-degree (Farenheit) temperature dispelled the notion that the planet was the earth's twin.

Pope John XXIII dies and is succeeded by Pope Paul VI.

The Arts

The best picture of the year is *Tom Jones*. Sidney Poitier is the best actor for his role in *Lilies of the Field*. Patricia Neal wins the best actress Oscar for her work in *Hud*. Other important films are Fellini's *8½* and Ian Fleming's *Dr. No*.

Three of the year's best selling books are J. D. Salinger's *Raise High the Roof Beam Carpenters, and Seymour—An Introduction*, Richard McKenna's *The Sand Pebbles*, and Mary McCarthy's *The Group*.

Jazz achieves greater recognition as an art form. Some of the most recognized performers are trumpet player Miles Davis; saxophone players John Coltrane and Sonny Rollins; pianists Bill Evans and Thelonious Monk; and the Modern Jazz Quartet.

Playwright Edward Albee receives much recognition for his disturbing play, *Who's Afraid of Virginia Woolf?*

Television

There are now over 56 million TV sets in American homes. The average family watches over six hours of TV daily.

Top rated shows of 1963 include "The Beverly Hillbillies," "The Andy Griffith Show," "The Red Skelton Show," "Ben Casey," and "Candid Camera."

Important news events take up an increasing amount of TV air time. The new Telstar satellites permit almost unlimited live broadcasting from around the world.

Sports

The Los Angeles Dodgers sweep the New York Yankees in four straight games to win the 1963 World Series. Dodger pitching ace Sandy Koufax strikes out 15 batters in the first game—a World Series record.

Heavyweight champion Sonny Liston knocks out Floyd Patterson in the first round of a title fight in Las Vegas.

An up-and-coming heavyweight boxer, Cassius Clay, knocks out English boxer Henry Cooper.

The Chicago Bears defeat the New York Giants 14 to 10 in frozen Wrigley field and capture the NFL title.

Fads and Fashion

Elizabeth Taylor and Richard Burton become the main source of Hollywood gossip. Although they are both married to others, their activities during the filming of *Cleopatra* start a series of international rumors. Eventually, the couple announce their marriage.

Two-button men's suits begin to outsell the traditional three-button models. Colors are a little brighter this year, favoring blues and light browns.

Women's clothes begin to borrow from the shapes and fabrics of men's garments. Boots are particularly popular in 1963.

TOP ROCK 'N' ROLL RECORDS OF 1963

Song	Artist	Record Label
Anyone Who Had a Heart	Dionne Warwick	Sceptor
Baby Workout	Jackie Wilson	Brunswick
Busted	Ray Charles	ABC

Song	Artist	Record Label
Candy Girl	The Four Seasons	Vee Jay
Come and Get These Memories	Martha and the Vandellas	Gordy
Da Doo Ron Ron	The Crystals	Philles
Don't Make Me Over	Dionne Warwick	Sceptor
Fingertips (Parts I & II)	Little Stevie Wonder	Tamla
For Your Precious Love	Garnett Minna and the Enchanters	United Artists
Heat Wave	Martha and the Vandellas	Gordy
Hello Stranger	Barbara Lewis	Atlantic
He's So Fine	The Chiffons	Laurie
Hey Girl	Freddy Scott	Colbix
Hey Paul	Paul and Paula	Phillips
If You Need Me	Wilson Pickett	DoubleL
If You Want to Be Happy	Jimmy Soul	SPQR
It's All Right	The Impressions	ABC
It's My Party	Leslie Gore	Mercury
Judy's Turn to Cry	Leslie Gore	Mercury
Land of a Thousand Dances	Chris Kenner	Instant
Louie Louie	The Kingsmen	Ward
Mean Woman Blues	Roy Orbison	Monument
Memphis	Lonnie Mack	Fraternity
Mickey's Monkey	Smokey Robinson and the Miracles	Tamla
Mockingbird	Inez Fox	Saturn
My Boyfriend's Back	The Angels	Smash
Our Day Will Come	Ruby and the Romantics	Capp
Pain in My Heart	Otis Redding	Volt
Pride and Joy	Marvin Gaye	Tamla
Sally Go Round the Roses	The Jaynettes	Tuff
South Street	Orleans	Cameo
Surfin' U.S.A.	The Beach Boys	Capitol
The Bird is the Word	Rivington	Liberty
These Arms of Mine	Otis Redding	Volt
Two Lovers	Mary Wells	Motown
Walk Like a Man	The Four Seasons	Vee Jay
When the Lovelight Starts Shining Through His Eyes	The Supremes	Motown
Wipeout	The Surfers	Dot
You Can't Sit Down	The Dovells	Cameo
You Don't Own Me	Leslie Gore	Mercury

Song	Artist	Record Label
You Really Got a Hold on Me	Smokey Robinson and the Miracles	Tamla
Zip-A-Dee-Doo-Dah	Bob B. Soxx and the Blue Jeans	Philles

A Final Note

Bobby Robinson—One Man's View of Rock 'n' Roll

Bobby Robinson is an important figure in the development of rock 'n' roll. Although he never received the publicity or the financial rewards of Motown's Berry Gordy, he was one of the first black men to own an independent record label. His first record production was in 1951, an old standard called "Where Are You" by the Mellow Moods. In 1953, Robinson formed his first label, Red Robin. During the next ten years, he was responsible for a number of important hits on a series of small labels. He originally concentrated on recording doo-wop groups in the early fifties and was involved in the making of several classics in this style. The two best-known songs were "Desirie," by the Charts, and "The Closer You Are," by the Channels (which he also helped write). In the WCBS-FM listeners poll of 1977, "Desirie" was the number nine all-time favorite record, while "The Closer You Are" was number sixteen. A measure of Robinson's importance is that he was the only record producer, aside from the Beatles' George Martin, to have two records in the top twenty.

Although he was based in New York, Robinson was interested in recording a wide variety of rock 'n' roll styles. At times, he would travel to another city to get a particular sound. For example, he recorded singer Lee Dorsey in his native New Orleans. In a two-day visit with the singer, Robinson co-wrote the hit song, "Ya Ya," and cut the record in an authentic New Orleans style. Robinson also had a hit with another New Orleans singer named Bobby Marchan, who was the original lead singer with Huey "Piano" Smith and the Clowns. In 1960, Marchan had an unusual hit with a song called "There Is Something on Your Mind."

Bobby Robinson was interested in all authentic forms of black music. As guitarist-record collector Billy Vera remarked, "Bobby just recorded anything out there that he thought was good—gospel, blues, New Orleans, doo-wop—just about anything that was real." A look at Robinson's impressive list of productions proves this to be true. In 1959, he recorded "Kansas City" by Wilbert Harrison and managed to have one of the only authentic blues hits of the fifties. The following year, Robinson produced yet another blues hit on Fire Records, "Fannie Mae," by Buster Brown. Several other well respected blues singers recorded for Robinson's Fire/Fury Records. The best known was Chicago bluesman Elmore James, who had several R&B hits in the early sixties.

Robinson understood the coming influence of gospel music at an early stage. He recorded gospel style hits with Gladys Knight and the Pips—"Every Beat of My Heart"—and Don Gardner and Dee Dee Ford—"I Need Your Loving." Unlike many of the elaborate Motown productions, these records had sparse instrumentation and a raw quality. "I Need Your Loving," in particular, had few lyrics and the quality of a church sermon. The record opened with Gardner shouting, "Woo-woo-woo woo-woo-woo-woo," and the two singers answered, "I need your lovin' every day." Robinson, who co-wrote the song, had devised this shout type of feeling. This record was one of the earlier examples of soul music. Around the same time, Robinson produced King Curtis's "Soul Twist," one of the better dance records of that era.

In addition to his many credits as a producer and a songwriter, Bobby Robinson has just about the best rounded view of rock 'n' roll of anybody on the scene. He is respected and admired by those who are interested in the development of authentic rock 'n' roll. Early in 1978, radio station WBAI ran eight hours of interviews and discussions with Robinson. WBAI is New York's only listener-sponsored station. Many of their announcers have an almost fanatical interest in authentic forms of American music. These people sincerely believe that these forms—jazz, gospel, blues, R&B, and rock 'n' roll—are the greatest examples of American culture. Robinson has had intimate contact with almost all of these forms. He is an extremely well-spoken man, who has countless stories and insights concerning the history of rock 'n' roll. In several interviews, Bobby shared many of his experiences with this writer.

BOBBY ROBINSON: IN CONVERSATION

Q. How did you first get involved in the music business?

A. I was a poor kid in South Carolina. My father was a poor truck farmer, and I guess my life was pretty lonely. But there were always a few guys around singing or playing music, which I loved. When I was around twenty, I moved to New York. I worked at different jobs for a while, and then joined the army. While I was in the army, I noticed that there was a lack of entertainment, so I put a show together which became very popular. When I returned to New York after the war, I looked for a business that was related to music. I wound up buying this little record store on 125th Street in Harlem. The store was midway beween the Apollo Theater, which was in its heyday, and Frank's Restaurant, where all the entertainers ate. All the big names often stopped into the store to see how well their records were selling. In this way, I got to know just about every R&B performer in the business.

Q. When did you get involved in record producing?

A. In 1951, I recorded my first record with the Mellow Moods. I really didn't know anything about the record business, except that I wanted to be in it. By 1953, I had my own label (Red Robin). The main thing at that time was vocal groups, so that's what I concentrated on. Some of my early records were by the Vocalaires ("Be True"), the Velvets ("I Cried"), the Scarlets ("Dear One"), who later became the Five Satins, the Rainbows ("Mary Lou"), and several others. At one point, I had thirteen doo-wop groups. Many of these records became local R&B hits. Even though many of these groups were only one-shots, they each had an original sound—their own sound.

Q. What was the atmosphere that led to that kind of a sound?

A. In those days, there was a sharp division between the three segments of music—R&B, country and western, and pop. There was very little crossover from one segment into the other. It was especially rare for an R&B artist to have a pop hit. There were lots of artists around who were being played on the black stations— Louis Jordan, Buddy Johnson and his Walking Rhythm Band. There were also ballad-blues and deep-blues singers who were popular in the R&B market. There were plenty of vocal groups around in the early fifties, but they weren't getting recorded.

Almost all of the group singers came from a background in gospel music. When I was a kid in the South, every church community had a half-dozen cappella singing groups. In fact, my cousins and I had one of these groups. Since there was no instrumental backing, the groups had to develop a strong vocal sound. So you see, the music had been there for many years, but there was no commercial exposure.

Q. How did Alan Freed affect all of this?

A. Alan Freed introduced black music to the mass white audience. These people had not been aware of this music, so many of them thought that Freed invented it. But that wasn't so.

Q. What about this music made it so popular in the fifties?

A. It had always been popular among blacks out of necessity. People in the rural South created this music for expression and enjoyment. The bare necessity to bring joy and entertain is the greatest hotbed for creativity. The music was popular among the black masses way before Alan Freed. But since it was new to the much larger white masses, it made a large impact. They picked up on the excitement and appeal that had always been there. But now, the natural and basic qualities of the music were being enjoyed by a much larger audience.

Q. What about the emotional and sexual qualities of the music?

A. Black music had so much more real feeling compared to the white pop music of that era. Kids didn't know exactly what it was they were hearing, but something was getting to them on a gut level. There was something in this music that implied a different way of expressing emotions.

Q. When did the expression "doo-wop" come about?

A. I'm not sure exactly when it came about. Since there was instrumental background, the groups would set their own beat. Doo-wop was one of the sounds that the bass singer made to create the beat, and I guess it just stuck. Originally, it was an ad-libbed sound that people began to use to describe the music.

Q. Many people talk about the relation between rock 'n' roll and the sexual revolution. How do you feel about this?

A. I want to say that the fifties was the beginning of the white sexual revolution. Most of the white population in America was middle class, but blacks were mostly ghetto or lower class. Many black people were quite poor and living in very close quarters. When you're forced to share the same bathroom and bedroom with different people, sex and closeness take on a different meaning. So the music of blacks expressed the sexuality and closeness that was missing in middle-class life. That's why white popular music didn't come to grips with these basic emotions. It was bland, easy listening, carefree, floating. The era of doo-wop and rock 'n' roll created an awakening of these feelings in young white people.

Q. How do you feel about the many street corner white groups that came along in the fifties?

A. For the most part, they were not really creative. They had never been exposed to a nitty-gritty type of life. You only create out of what you have experienced. I really believe that a soul singer cannot be authentic without a church background or a hard way of life. They say, "the hardest wheel has been through the hottest furnace."

Q. What are you feelings about the current fifties revival?

A. I recently recorded a two-record set of the Drifters and the Coasters. We were doing the original tunes and trying to capture the original feel. But I find it almost impossible to recreate the authentic feel of a hit record. For the most part, these weren't the original group members, although they were good singers. But a hit record is a piece of magic, where everything blends and falls into place with both the singers and musicians. It's pretty hard to duplicate that quality fifteen years later. Every creative act has its own time and its own magic. But I'll tell you something about the revival of fifties music. I think that many of these old records would really go over today if they were done in the original style with a little better recording technique. I get a lot of kids coming into my store and asking for slow records, so I guess there may be something to the revival. I think things may have gotten too permissive, and kids would like to go back to the days before the sexual revolution.

Q. Whom do you consider the most important performer of the fifties? Whose work holds up best?

A. Sam Cooke ... I guess I'm also counting some of his gospel work with the Soul Stirrers. Sam's father was a storefront preacher in Chicago. He used to have his family back him up. The Soul Stirrers were already very famous. When they heard Sam sing, they convinced old man Cooke to let him join the group. Sam was so young, and such a natural talent, that the group became bigger than ever. I knew Sam pretty well, because the Soul Stirrers often worked in Harlem. I had been trying to convince him to become a popular singer. One night, I went back to his room at the Cecil Hotel. He said he had this original song that he wanted to play for me. The room was crowded with girls and fellas, so me and Sam went into the men's room. We locked the door, and Sam played "You Send Me," while he accompanied himself on acoustic guitar.

After I heard him sing "You Send Me," I said, "Make the move right now. You've got an original sound that hasn't been heard yet in popular music. There are guys copying your sound. They are sitting in their rooms night and day and trying to imitate what you do. The first one to hit the street is going to make it big, and it will be too late for you." He said, "Bobby, I'm making two hundred dollars a week, which supports my family. The gospel audience is funny. They consider me a religious person. If I become a pop singer and fail, they might not take me back. What will I do then, get a broom and sweep the streets?" I said, "Sam, I appreciate your feelings, but I'm telling you that there is absolutely no way you can miss."

I finally had him convinced to make the big move. He said, "O.K., Bobby, let's do it." He was going on the road for two weeks, and we had decided to record "You Send Me" after he came back. But he was signed to his record company as an individual artist as well as a member of the Soul Stirrers. Not surprisingly, they wouldn't let him out of his contract. They said, "If you're going to sing rock 'n' roll, it's going to be for us." So they set up a company around Sam, and "You Send Me" became a multimillion seller.

Q. Whom do you consider the first authentic rock 'n' roll performer?

A. To my mind, Little Richard was the real forerunner of rock 'n' roll. His style was a combination of gospel fervor and the beat.

In churches throughout the South, we call this "the Baptist beat." Those churches were too poor to have a piano or organ, but the music was the greatest I had ever heard in my whole life. To me, the greatest music is not made with sophisticated background. When there's too much going on in the background, singers tend to lay back. But in those days, you had to make your own feeling. That Baptist beat was really electric. It would start with a single hand clap and move to a double hand clap. That's the same beat that is used in rock 'n' roll.

Little Richard made the same kind of music as the Baptist church congregations. He used the band to do the same things the congregation did with their hands, feet, and voices. Of course, he changed the words to suit the kids. But if you ever go into a southern Baptist church, you'll hear the same kind of feel.

Q. How do you see the role of Elvis in rock 'n' roll?

A. He was a great artist. Although he was white, he was a product of a similar environment as southern blacks. He grew up in the same area and worked side by side with blacks in trucks and in the mills. Even though he copied men like Crudup, he definitely had his own original style. He admits that Crudup was his mentor. Elvis's first record was a Crudup song, "That's All Right Mamma." But Crudup never got compensated for writing the song. His story is like a lot of the early bluesmen.

Crudup was signed to me late in his career. Although his name appears on the song, he never got paid. There was a guy named Lester Melrose who would record any bluesmen who came to him on an old wire recorder. He also published the songs that these men recorded. Arthur "Big Boy" Crudup was a migrant farmer—a troubador who understood nothing about copyright laws. During the summers, he picked oranges in Florida. Winters, he would go to Virginia and pick vegetables. He played and sang here and there, but had no understanding of the music business.

At some point, Lester Melrose sold his publishing rights to a well-known New York publishing company, Hill and Range Music. They split the royalties with Presley's publishing company, but Crudup didn't get a dime. Because I was working with him, I decided to try and sue Hill and Range. The writer's royalties on a Presley record would amount to thousands of dollars each year. Hill and Range agreed to make a settlement of about $13,000.

Crudup flew into New York with his sons. This was probably more money than they had seen in their entire lives. At the last minute, Hill and Range backed out. They decided that it would cost them less money to go to court. That was the end of it. I think Crudup got some tiny amount like $1,600. A few years later, he died penniless.

There was another man who influenced Elvis even more than Crudup. Otis Blackwell was a New York songwriter who wrote Presley hits like "Don't Be Cruel" and "All Shook Up." Otis would make a demo of the song, and Presley would copy his singing performance exactly. Unlike Crudup, Blackwell made quite a bit of money in songwriting royalties. But in order to get his songs recorded, he had to agree to make Elvis a cowriter. There was even an article about this in *The Village Voice* recently. Otis is finally getting some of the recognition that he deserves. But he could have used it more back then.

Q. What are your feelings about the current state of popular music?

A. I'm not at all happy with the current music scene. Back in the fifties, there were so many good singers and good tunes. You just went into the studio, put the right ingredients together, and hoped for some magic. But now everyone is so involved with big studios and big orchestras. There just seems to be a lack of good basic music. I think producers and artists have to get back to fundamentals. A strong tune and a good singer are still what it's all about. You can go just so far with a complicated arrangement and complicated recording equipment. Right now, I think they have gone too far. I think the public will soon be ready for a more basic and honest kind of music, but we'll have to wait and see what happens.

Appendix

COMPILATION ALBUMS

Many of the single records discussed in this book are available on fine compilation albums. Several of these are listed below:

16 King-Sized Rhythm & Blues Hits—Columbia
Rock & Roll Forever, Volume I—Atlantic
This Is How It All Began—Specialty
Original Golden Hits of the Great Groups—Mercury
Sun's Gold Hits—Sun
History of Rhythm and Blues, Volumes I–IV—Atlantic
Your Old Favorites—Old Town
The Fifties' Greatest Hits—Columbia
Collector's Records of the 50's and 60's—Laurie
Anthology of Rhythm and Blues—Columbia

A SAMPLER OF TEENAGE SLANG

chug-a-lug—finishing an entire beverage in one gulp. Particularly popular in college fraternity, beer-drinking contests.
duck-tail—also known as d.a. A haircut that featured long sideburns that tailed off in the back like the rear end of a duck.
going ape—getting really excited over someone or something, and showing it.
going steady—the teenage equivalent of marriage. A vow to date only that one person.
going steadily—less of a commitment than going steady. Two

teenagers who are going out mainly with each other, but not exclusively.

hip—also cool or hep. Someone who is fashionable and up to date, or with it.

let's run it up the flagpole and see who salutes—another way of saying, let's try it out and see if it works.

nuggie—punching someone in the head with one's knuckles in a playful manner. The act is half affectionate and very painful.

rock—also called greaser in some areas. Tough looking teenage boys who love rock 'n' roll, motorcycle jackets, and d.a. haircuts.

square—also called an L7 or a cube in severe cases. Somebody with old-fashioned ideas. Not keeping up with the trends of the in-crowd.

with-it—someone who is attuned to the latest fashions. The opposite of a square.

A GLOSSARY OF ROCK 'N' ROLL TERMS

arranger—a person who writes out the musical parts to be played or sung at a recording session or live performance.

blues-based—music which is derived from the forms and feelings of this fundamental style of Afro-American music.

b/w—an abbreviation for backed with. Most single records have an A and B side. The A side is generally considered to be more important, although a number of B sides became big hits.

country and western (C&W)—a type of white folk music which developed mainly in the southern sections of the U.S. Originally known as hillbilly music, the major centers for the sound are Memphis and Nashville.

cover record—a copy made of an original record. During the fifties it often referred to a white artist on a major label copying a record of a black artist on a small, independent label.

demo—a demonstration record. Demos are usually not intended to be released as a finished product, although many rock 'n' roll hits were originally intended as demos.

melisma—the stretching of a sound over one note—a common device used by gospel style singers.

Motown—a nickname for Detroit, or motor town. The sound, which developed at the labels owned by Berry Gordy, combined rhythm and blues with pop. Some of the most important artists on this label include Marvin Gaye, Diana Ross, and Stevie Wonder.

pop—originally used to describe the music which was popular with the majority of white American adults. Because rock has been completely absorbed into popular music, the term has been replaced by the description, middle of the road (MOR).

producer—in some cases, the person who puts up the money to make a record. Often, the producer runs the entire record session—functioning much like the director of a film.

rhythm and blues (R&B)—a general description of the black musical market. An extension of basic blues forms which occurred when rural self-accompanied musicians migrated to urban areas and added bands.

riff—a musical phrase which is repeated throughout a song.

soul music—a type of R&B which emphasizes the influences of black gospel music. In the mid-sixties the term became linked to the integration movement and "black pride."

wall of sound—a type of recording originally developed by producer Phil Spector. It uses dense orchestrations and voices to create an effect of power and tension—the music engulfs the listener.

MUSIC BUSINESS TRADE MAGAZINES

Billboard Magazine, Los Angeles, California
Cashbox Magazine, New York, New York
Record World Magazine, New York, New York

Bibliography

Belz, Carl. *The Story of Rock.* New York, N.Y.: Oxford University Press, 1969.

Berman, Jay. *The Fifties Book.* Berkeley, California: Medallion Books, 1974.

Clark, Dick. *Rock, Roll and Remember.* New York: Popular Library, 1976.

Erlich, Lillian. *What Jazz Is All About.* New York: Julian Messner, 1975.

Gillett, Charlie. *The Sound of the City.* New York: Outerbridge and Dienstfrey, 1970.

Grossman, Lloyd. *A Social History of Rock Music.* New York: David McKay, 1976.

Lackman, Ron. *Remember Television.* New York: G. P. Putnam, 1971.

Malone, Bill. *Country Music U.S.A.* Austin, Texas: University of Texas Press, 1968.

Marcus, Greil. *Mystery Train.* New York: Dutton, 1976.

Miller and Nowack. *The Fifties: The Way We Really Were.* New York: Doubleday, 1976.

Nite, Norm N. *Rock On.* New York: Thomas Y. Crowell, 1974.

Rhode, H. *The Gold of Rock and Roll, 1955–1967.* New York: Arbor House, 1970.

Ribakove, Barbara, and Ribakove, Sy. *The Nifty Fifties.* New York: Universal Award, 1974.

The Rolling Stone Illustrated History of Rock and Roll. Edited by Jim Miller. New York: Random House Books–Rolling Stone Press, 1976.

The Rolling Stone Rock 'n' Roll Reader. Edited by Ben Fong Torres. New York: Bantam Books, 1974.

Saan, Paul. *Fads, Follies and Delusions of the American People.*
   New York: Crown Publishing Co., 1967.
Shaw, Arnold. *The Rock Revolution.* New York: The Macmillan
   Co., 1969.
————. *The Rockin' Fifties.* New York: Hawthorn Books, 1970.
————. *The World of Soul.* New Jersey: Cowles Book Co., 1970.
Time Life Books: 1950–1960. New York: Time Life, Inc.
Whitburn, Joel. *Record Research,* based on *Billboard* magazine,
   1949–71.

Index

ABOUT THE AUTHOR

I was born in Brooklyn, New York, and grew up with fifties rock 'n' roll. I began playing in bands in the late fifties, experimenting with both jazz and R&B. By the early sixties, I had done some recording, as well as backup work with a number of well-known groups. These included the Platters, the Jive Five, and Vito and the Salutations. At the same time, I attended as many of the major rock 'n' roll shows as I possibly could.

I attended the City College of New York, where I majored in psychology on both the bachelor's and master's levels. At the same time, I continued to play as many dances and record sessions as time allowed. During the sixties, I played and recorded with several successful East Coast bands. One of these groups—Sweet Stavin Chain—opened for many of rock's most well-known acts, including Cream, Chicago, Van Morrison, and B. B. King.

It's Rock 'n' Roll is my first book. I am currently working on another book, "The Superstars of Rock." I have also written various magazine articles over the past few years and continue to remain active as a musician, songwriter, and music teacher in New York City.